Mastering

DevOps

Concepts, Techniques, and Applications

Nikhilesh Mishra,
Author

Website
https://www.nikhileshmishra.com

Copyright Information

Dedication

This book is lovingly dedicated to the cherished memory of my father, **Late Krishna Gopal Mishra**, and my mother**, Mrs. Vijay Kanti Mishra.** Their unwavering support, guidance, and love continue to inspire me.

Table of Contents

Author's Preface

Welcome to the captivating world of the knowledge we are about to explore! Within these pages, we invite you to embark on a journey that delves into the frontiers of information and understanding.

Charting the Path to Knowledge

Dive deep into the subjects we are about to explore as we unravel the intricate threads of innovation, creativity, and problem-solving. Whether you're a curious enthusiast, a seasoned professional, or an eager learner, this book serves as your gateway to gaining a deeper understanding.

Your Guiding Light

From the foundational principles of our chosen field to the advanced frontiers of its applications, we've meticulously crafted this book to be your trusted companion. Each chapter is an expedition, guided by expertise and filled with practical insights to empower you on your quest for knowledge.

What Awaits You

- **Illuminate the Origins:** Embark on a journey through the historical evolution of our chosen field, discovering key milestones that have paved the way for breakthroughs.

- **Demystify Complex Concepts:** Grasp the fundamental principles, navigate intricate concepts, and explore practical applications.

- **Mastery of the Craft:** Equip yourself with the skills and knowledge needed to excel in our chosen domain.

Your Journey Begins Here

As we embark on this enlightening journey together, remember that mastery is not just about knowledge but also the wisdom to apply it. Let each chapter be a stepping stone towards unlocking your potential, and let this book be your guide to becoming a true connoisseur of our chosen field.

So, turn the page, delve into the chapters, and immerse yourself in the world of knowledge. Let curiosity be your compass, and let the pursuit of understanding be your guide.

Begin your expedition now. Your quest for mastery awaits!

Sincerely,

Nikhilesh Mishra,

Author

CHAPTER 1

Introduction to DevOps

In the fast-paced world of modern software development, the need for agility, collaboration, and efficiency has never been greater. Enter DevOps – a groundbreaking approach that has revolutionized the way software is developed, delivered, and maintained. DevOps is more than just a buzzword; it's a culture, a set of practices, and a collection of powerful tools that have transformed the IT industry.

In this chapter, we embark on a journey into the heart of DevOps, where we will explore its origins, fundamental principles, and the core concepts that underpin its philosophy. We'll delve into the driving forces behind the rise of DevOps, uncovering why it's not merely a trend but a fundamental shift in how organizations deliver value to their customers. Whether you're a seasoned IT professional looking to deepen your knowledge or a newcomer eager to grasp the essence of DevOps, this chapter is your gateway to a world where collaboration and automation reign supreme. So, let's embark on this enlightening journey into the realm of DevOps and discover how it's reshaping the software development landscape.

A. Definition and Evolution of DevOps

In the world of technology and software development, the term "DevOps" has become ubiquitous, representing a transformative approach that has redefined how organizations build, deploy, and manage software. DevOps is not just a methodology; it's a cultural shift, a set of practices, and a philosophy that seeks to bridge the historically siloed domains of software development and IT operations. To truly understand DevOps, we must explore its definition and trace its evolution.

Defining DevOps

DevOps, a portmanteau of "development" and "operations," can be defined as a set of practices, principles, and cultural philosophies that emphasize collaboration, communication, and automation between software development (Dev) and IT operations (Ops) teams. Its primary goal is to streamline and accelerate the software development and delivery process while ensuring a higher level of quality and reliability.

Key components of the DevOps definition include:

1. **Collaboration:** DevOps encourages close collaboration between development and operations teams. This collaboration aims to break down traditional organizational silos, fostering shared responsibility for the entire software delivery lifecycle.

2. **Automation:** Automation is a central pillar of DevOps. It involves automating repetitive tasks, such as code integration, testing, deployment, and infrastructure provisioning, to reduce human error, increase efficiency, and speed up the release cycle.

3. **Continuous Integration and Continuous Deployment (CI/CD):** CI/CD pipelines are essential in DevOps. Continuous Integration involves frequently merging code changes into a shared repository, while Continuous Deployment automates the deployment of code changes to production environments as soon as they pass automated tests.

4. **Monitoring and Feedback:** DevOps places a strong emphasis on monitoring applications and infrastructure in real-time. This feedback loop enables teams to identify issues promptly, make data-driven decisions, and continuously improve their processes.

The Evolution of DevOps

DevOps didn't emerge overnight; it evolved over several decades in response to the challenges and inefficiencies in traditional software development and IT operations. Here's a brief overview of its evolution:

1. **Waterfall Model (Pre-DevOps Era):** Before DevOps, software development typically followed the Waterfall model,

a linear and sequential approach that often led to lengthy release cycles, communication gaps, and high failure rates.

2. **Agile Manifesto (Early 2000s):** The Agile Manifesto introduced a more flexible and collaborative approach to software development, emphasizing individuals and interactions over processes and tools. Agile methodologies laid the foundation for DevOps by promoting iterative development and customer-centricity.

3. **Infrastructure as Code (IaC) and Automation (Mid-2000s):** The mid-2000s saw the emergence of Infrastructure as Code (IaC) and automation tools like Puppet and Chef. These technologies allowed for the automated provisioning and management of infrastructure, setting the stage for DevOps practices.

4. **The DevOps Movement (Late 2000s):** DevOps gained momentum as organizations recognized the need to align development and operations to deliver software faster and with higher quality. Influential books, conferences, and community-driven practices emerged to promote DevOps adoption.

5. **DevOps Tools and Ecosystem (2010s):** The DevOps ecosystem expanded with the introduction of tools like Docker for containerization, Jenkins for continuous integration, Kubernetes for container orchestration, and a myriad of other

automation and monitoring solutions.

6. **DevOps Culture and Continuous Improvement (Present):** Today, DevOps is not just about tools and practices; it's about fostering a culture of continuous improvement, collaboration, and learning. Organizations are increasingly embracing DevOps as a way to stay competitive and meet the demands of a rapidly evolving digital landscape.

As we delve deeper into this book, we will explore the key concepts, practices, and tools that define the DevOps movement, empowering you to harness its potential and drive transformation within your own organization. DevOps is not a static destination; it's a journey of evolution and improvement that enables businesses to innovate and thrive in the digital age.

B. Key Concepts in DevOps: Continuous Integration, Continuous Deployment, and Automation

DevOps is characterized by a set of core concepts and practices that aim to streamline software development, enhance collaboration, and accelerate the delivery of high-quality software. Among these foundational concepts, Continuous Integration (CI), Continuous Deployment (CD), and Automation stand out as crucial pillars of the DevOps philosophy.

Continuous Integration (CI)

Continuous Integration is a development practice that involves frequently integrating code changes from multiple contributors into a shared code repository. The primary objectives of CI are to detect and address integration issues early in the development process and to ensure that the codebase remains consistently functional.

Key Aspects of CI:

1. **Frequent Code Integration:** Developers commit code changes to the central repository multiple times a day. This approach contrasts with traditional development methods that involve infrequent, large-scale code integrations.

2. **Automated Testing:** CI systems automatically trigger a battery of tests (unit tests, integration tests, etc.) upon code submission. These tests help identify bugs and issues promptly, preventing them from propagating to subsequent stages.

3. **Fast Feedback Loop:** Developers receive immediate feedback on the quality and compatibility of their code changes. This rapid feedback loop promotes accountability and encourages developers to maintain high code quality standards.

4. **Version Control:** CI relies on robust version control systems (e.g., Git) to manage code repositories. This ensures that developers work with the most up-to-date codebase and can easily track changes.

Continuous Deployment (CD)

Continuous Deployment is an extension of CI that focuses on automating the deployment process of code changes to production environments. It goes beyond continuous integration by automatically releasing code to production if it passes all tests and quality checks.

Key Aspects of CD:

1. **Automated Deployment Pipeline:** CD pipelines are designed to automate the entire software delivery process, from code integration to production deployment. This minimizes the need for manual intervention and reduces the risk of human error.

2. **Incremental Updates:** CD promotes small, incremental updates to production, which allows for faster feature delivery and quicker bug fixes.

3. **Rollback Mechanisms:** In the event of issues or errors in the production environment, CD pipelines typically include rollback mechanisms that can quickly revert to a stable version

of the application.

4. **Monitoring and Feedback Loops:** CD relies on real-time monitoring and feedback to ensure that deployed code performs as expected in the production environment. Any deviations from the expected behavior trigger alerts and further actions.

Automation

Automation is at the core of DevOps, serving as a means to achieve efficiency, consistency, and repeatability in all aspects of the software development lifecycle.

Key Aspects of Automation in DevOps:

1. **Infrastructure Automation:** Infrastructure as Code (IaC) tools such as Terraform and Ansible enable the automated provisioning and configuration of infrastructure resources, reducing manual intervention and ensuring consistent environments across development, testing, and production.

2. **Deployment Automation:** Deployment scripts and containerization technologies like Docker simplify the process of packaging and deploying applications to various environments, making it possible to replicate deployment procedures accurately and rapidly.

3. **Testing Automation:** Automated testing frameworks and

tools ensure that testing processes, including unit testing, integration testing, and load testing, can be executed consistently and swiftly.

4. **Monitoring and Alerting Automation:** DevOps teams rely on automated monitoring tools to track application performance, resource utilization, and security threats. Automated alerts and notifications help teams respond proactively to issues.

5. **Continuous Integration and Continuous Deployment (CI/CD):** CI/CD pipelines automate the building, testing, and deployment of code changes, minimizing manual intervention and reducing the time it takes to move code from development to production.

By embracing these key concepts of Continuous Integration, Continuous Deployment, and Automation, DevOps teams can achieve greater efficiency, faster time-to-market, improved software quality, and enhanced collaboration, ultimately delivering value to end-users and customers with greater agility and reliability. These concepts are the building blocks of a successful DevOps culture and practice.

C. DevOps Culture and Principles

DevOps is not merely a set of tools and practices; it is

fundamentally rooted in a culture of collaboration, communication, and continuous improvement. A strong DevOps culture is essential for organizations aiming to break down traditional silos, accelerate software delivery, and deliver higher-quality products. In this section, we will delve into the core principles and cultural aspects that underpin the DevOps movement.

1. Collaboration and Communication:

- **Cross-Functional Teams:** DevOps encourages the formation of cross-functional teams that include developers, operations personnel, testers, and other stakeholders. These teams work together throughout the software development lifecycle (SDLC).

- **Shared Responsibility:** In a DevOps culture, everyone shares responsibility for the success of the software delivery process. Developers, operations, and other team members collaborate to ensure that code moves smoothly from development through testing and into production.

- **Open Communication:** DevOps fosters open and transparent communication. Teams regularly exchange information, feedback, and ideas, reducing misunderstandings and improving decision-making.

2. Automation:

- **Automating Repetitive Tasks:** DevOps principles emphasize automating repetitive and manual tasks to minimize human error, increase efficiency, and accelerate the delivery pipeline. This includes automating testing, deployment, infrastructure provisioning, and more.

- **Infrastructure as Code (IaC):** IaC is a key component of automation, allowing infrastructure resources to be defined and managed through code. Tools like Terraform and Ansible enable the automation of infrastructure provisioning and configuration.

- **CI/CD Pipelines:** Continuous Integration (CI) and Continuous Deployment (CD) pipelines automate the building, testing, and deployment of code changes, ensuring that new features and updates can be delivered rapidly and reliably.

3. Continuous Improvement:

- **Kaizen Philosophy:** DevOps embraces the Kaizen philosophy, which emphasizes continuous improvement. Teams regularly review their processes, identify bottlenecks, and seek opportunities to optimize and enhance their workflows.

- **Feedback Loops:** DevOps relies on feedback loops to gather data on application performance, user behavior, and system stability. This data informs decision-making and drives ongoing improvements.

4. Empowerment and Trust:

- **Empowered Teams:** DevOps encourages teams to take ownership of their work and make decisions autonomously. This empowerment fosters a sense of ownership and accountability among team members.

- **Trust:** Trust is a fundamental principle of DevOps culture. Team members trust each other to perform their roles effectively, make informed decisions, and collaborate towards shared goals.

5. Measurement and Metrics:

- **Key Performance Indicators (KPIs):** DevOps teams establish KPIs and metrics to measure the performance of their processes and systems. This data-driven approach helps identify areas for improvement and ensures that decisions are based on evidence.

- **Continuous Monitoring:** DevOps promotes continuous monitoring of applications and infrastructure. Real-time data and alerts enable teams to proactively address issues, minimizing downtime and service disruptions.

6. Security Integration (DevSecOps):

- **Security as Code:** DevOps integrates security practices throughout the SDLC. Security measures are treated as code and are automated and validated alongside other development and operational processes.

- **Identity and Access Management:** DevOps teams implement robust identity and access management controls to protect sensitive resources and ensure compliance with security standards.

7. Lean Thinking:

- **Eliminating Waste:** DevOps applies lean thinking principles to eliminate waste, reduce manual efforts, and optimize resource utilization. This results in faster delivery times and cost savings.

8. Cultural Transformation:

- **Leadership Support:** Successful DevOps transformations require strong leadership support. Leaders set the tone for cultural change and must actively champion DevOps principles and practices.

- **Overcoming Resistance:** Resistance to change is common in organizations. DevOps initiatives address this by providing training, education, and support to help individuals and teams adapt to new ways of working.

DevOps culture is not something that can be achieved overnight; it requires time, commitment, and a continuous focus on improvement. Organizations that embrace these principles and cultivate a DevOps culture position themselves to respond to market changes more effectively, deliver better products, and thrive in today's fast-paced, digital-driven landscape.

D. Benefits and Challenges of DevOps

DevOps, with its focus on collaboration, automation, and continuous improvement, offers numerous benefits to organizations seeking to streamline their software development and delivery processes. However, like any transformative approach, it also presents its own set of challenges. Let's explore the significant benefits and challenges associated with DevOps.

Benefits of DevOps:

1. **Accelerated Software Delivery:**

   - **Continuous Integration and Continuous Deployment (CI/CD):** DevOps automates the building, testing, and deployment of code changes, allowing organizations to release software updates faster and more frequently. This speed enables companies to respond to market demands rapidly.

2. **Improved Quality and Reliability:**

- **Automated Testing:** DevOps encourages comprehensive automated testing, reducing the likelihood of defects and improving software quality.

- **Continuous Monitoring:** Real-time monitoring and feedback loops help teams identify and resolve issues before they impact users, enhancing system reliability.

3. **Enhanced Collaboration:**

- **Cross-Functional Teams:** DevOps fosters collaboration among development, operations, and other stakeholders, breaking down traditional silos.

- **Communication:** Open communication channels improve understanding and alignment among team members.

4. **Efficiency and Cost Savings:**

- **Automation:** DevOps automation reduces manual, error-prone tasks, saving time and resources.

- **Resource Optimization:** Lean practices in DevOps

help organizations use resources more efficiently, reducing waste and cutting operational costs.

5. **Increased Scalability:**

- **Infrastructure as Code (IaC):** IaC allows organizations to scale infrastructure resources up or down as needed, adapting to changing workloads and demands.

6. **Enhanced Security (DevSecOps):**

- **Security Integration:** DevOps integrates security practices throughout the software development lifecycle, reducing vulnerabilities and enhancing data protection.

- **Compliance as Code:** Compliance checks can be automated, ensuring that applications adhere to regulatory requirements.

7. **Predictable Releases:**

- **Release Management:** DevOps provides a structured approach to release management, resulting in more predictable and less risky releases.

8. **Continuous Improvement:**

- **Kaizen Philosophy:** DevOps embraces a culture of

continuous improvement, enabling organizations to evolve their processes and adapt to changing business needs.

Challenges of DevOps:

1. **Cultural Transformation:**

   - **Resistance to Change:** Implementing a DevOps culture requires overcoming resistance to change, especially in organizations with long-standing traditions and practices.

2. **Complexity:**

   - **Tool Complexity:** Managing a variety of DevOps tools and technologies can be challenging. Teams need to select and integrate the right tools for their specific needs.

3. **Skill Gap:**

   - **Skill Development:** DevOps requires a broad skill set, including automation, scripting, cloud computing, and containerization. Teams may need to invest in training and skill development.

4. **Security Concerns:**

   - **Security Challenges:** Integrating security into

DevOps practices (DevSecOps) can be challenging, as it may require changes to existing security processes and toolsets.

5. **Coordination and Communication:**

- **Coordination Overhead:** Collaboration across teams can introduce coordination overhead, particularly in large organizations.

6. **Tool Integration:**

- **Tool Integration:** Integrating various DevOps tools and ensuring they work seamlessly together can be complex and time-consuming.

7. **Scalability and Standardization:**

- **Scaling DevOps:** Adapting DevOps practices to large-scale enterprise environments can be challenging. Standardization is crucial but may face resistance.

8. **Compliance and Governance:**

- **Compliance Challenges:** Maintaining compliance while implementing DevOps practices can be demanding, especially in highly regulated industries.

9. **Legacy Systems:**

- **Legacy Challenges:** Transitioning DevOps practices to legacy systems can be difficult due to technology and process constraints.

10. **Monitoring and Feedback:**

- **Data Overload:** Managing and interpreting the vast amount of data generated by continuous monitoring can be overwhelming.

11. **Tool and Technology Evolvement:**

- **Rapid Technological Change:** The DevOps landscape is constantly evolving, and keeping up with the latest tools and technologies can be challenging.

DevOps is a powerful approach that offers significant benefits to organizations striving for agility, efficiency, and high-quality software delivery. However, addressing the associated challenges requires careful planning, investment in skills development, and a commitment to cultural transformation. Ultimately, the rewards of DevOps—faster time-to-market, improved collaboration, and better software quality—far outweigh the challenges for many organizations.

CHAPTER 2

Introduction to DevOps Practices

In the dynamic realm of software development and IT operations, DevOps practices stand as the guiding principles that drive the transformation of traditional, siloed workflows into a harmonious, automated, and efficient ecosystem. These practices are the tangible manifestations of the DevOps culture, reflecting the core values of collaboration, continuous improvement, and streamlined processes.

In this section, we embark on a journey through the key DevOps practices that have revolutionized the way software is conceived, built, and delivered. From Continuous Integration (CI) and Continuous Deployment (CD) to Infrastructure as Code (IaC) and automated testing, we will explore each practice in-depth, unraveling their significance and demonstrating how they collectively propel organizations toward accelerated software delivery and enhanced product quality. By embracing and mastering these practices, you'll be equipped to navigate the DevOps landscape and drive innovation in your own development and operations endeavors. So, let's dive into the world of DevOps practices and discover how they are reshaping the future of technology.

A. Continuous Integration (CI): Streamlining Development with Automation

Continuous Integration (CI) is a fundamental DevOps practice that has revolutionized the way software is developed and delivered. At its core, CI is about automating the integration of code changes from multiple contributors into a shared code repository. This practice promotes collaboration, reduces integration issues, and accelerates the development process. In this in-depth exploration of CI, we will delve into its principles, benefits, and best practices.

Principles of Continuous Integration:

1. **Frequent Code Integration:** In a CI environment, developers integrate their code changes into a shared repository multiple times a day. This contrasts with traditional development methods, where integration occurs infrequently, leading to large, complex, and error-prone merges.

2. **Automated Testing:** CI relies heavily on automated testing. Upon each code submission, a CI system automatically triggers a battery of tests, including unit tests, integration tests, and even user acceptance tests. This ensures that changes do not introduce defects or regressions.

3. **Fast Feedback Loop:** Developers receive immediate feedback on the quality and compatibility of their code changes. If a test fails or if issues arise during the integration

process, developers can address them promptly. This rapid feedback loop encourages accountability and drives continuous improvement.

4. **Version Control:** CI relies on robust version control systems, such as Git, to manage code repositories. Version control ensures that developers work with the most up-to-date codebase and can easily track changes and their history.

Benefits of Continuous Integration:

1. **Reduced Integration Issues:** Frequent integration helps catch integration issues early in the development process, making them easier and less costly to fix. This reduces the risk of large, disruptive integration problems that can delay project timelines.

2. **Higher Software Quality:** Automated testing in CI ensures that code changes meet predefined quality standards. This results in higher software quality and a reduced likelihood of introducing bugs or regressions.

3. **Accelerated Development:** CI shortens the time between writing code and detecting issues. Developers can focus on coding rather than spending time on manual integration and testing tasks, which accelerates the development cycle.

4. **Enhanced Collaboration:** CI encourages collaboration

among developers, as they frequently integrate their code changes and resolve integration issues together. It fosters a sense of shared responsibility for the codebase.

5. **Risk Mitigation:** By continuously testing and integrating code changes, CI reduces the risk associated with large, untested code deployments. This mitigates the chances of critical production failures.

Best Practices for Continuous Integration:

1. **Automate Everything:** Automate the entire CI process, from code integration and building to testing and deployment. Use CI/CD tools like Jenkins, Travis CI, or CircleCI to orchestrate these automation tasks.

2. **Isolation of Environments:** Use containerization technologies like Docker to ensure that the CI environment closely matches the production environment, reducing the "it works on my machine" problem.

3. **Version Control:** Use a robust version control system like Git and enforce version control best practices, including code branching and tagging for releases.

4. **Parallel Testing:** To speed up the testing process, run tests in parallel across multiple environments and configurations.

5. **Immediate Feedback:** Set up notifications and alerts to

provide immediate feedback to developers when code integration or testing fails.

6. **Infrastructure as Code (IaC):** Automate the provisioning and configuration of test environments using IaC tools like Terraform or Ansible to ensure consistency.

7. **Regression Testing:** Implement comprehensive regression testing to ensure that code changes do not inadvertently break existing functionality.

Continuous Integration is a cornerstone of DevOps, transforming the way teams collaborate, code, and deliver software. By adhering to CI principles and best practices, organizations can accelerate their software development process, enhance quality, and respond to market demands with agility and confidence.

B. Continuous Deployment (CD): Streamlining Software Delivery and Release

Continuous Deployment (CD) is a vital DevOps practice that extends the principles of Continuous Integration (CI) to the next level. While CI focuses on automating the integration of code changes, CD takes automation a step further by automating the deployment of code changes into production environments. CD enables organizations to release new features and updates to their software applications rapidly, reliably, and with minimal manual intervention. In this in-depth exploration of CD, we'll delve into its principles, benefits, and best practices.

Principles of Continuous Deployment:

1. **Automated Deployment Pipeline:** CD relies on automated deployment pipelines, which are orchestrated sequences of actions and tests that automatically build, test, and deploy code changes. These pipelines are defined as code and are executed consistently for each code change.

2. **Incremental Updates:** CD promotes the idea of releasing software changes in small, incremental updates. This approach contrasts with traditional release cycles, where organizations may bundle numerous changes into infrequent, larger releases.

3. **Continuous Monitoring and Feedback:** After deploying code changes to production, CD includes continuous monitoring and feedback loops. Real-time monitoring ensures that applications perform as expected, and feedback mechanisms trigger alerts and further actions if issues arise.

4. **Rollback Mechanisms:** CD pipelines often include rollback mechanisms that allow teams to quickly revert to a stable version of the application in the event of issues or errors in the production environment.

Benefits of Continuous Deployment:

1. **Rapid Time-to-Market:** CD enables organizations to deliver new features, enhancements, and bug fixes to users quickly. This rapid time-to-market helps businesses respond to market demands and user feedback faster.

2. **Reduced Manual Intervention:** Automation in CD minimizes the need for manual deployment and reduces the risk of human errors during the release process. This results in more reliable releases.

3. **Enhanced Software Quality:** Because CD builds on the foundation of CI, code changes are thoroughly tested before reaching production. This enhances software quality and reduces the likelihood of introducing defects.

4. **Continuous Improvement:** CD promotes a culture of continuous improvement. Teams can quickly iterate on features and updates based on real-time feedback and data, leading to better products.

5. **Reduced Downtime:** Incremental updates and rollback mechanisms in CD minimize downtime and service disruptions. Even if an issue arises, it can often be resolved swiftly without affecting users significantly.

Best Practices for Continuous Deployment:

1. **Automate Everything:** Automate the entire deployment process, from code integration and testing to deployment and monitoring.

2. **Immutable Infrastructure:** Use immutable infrastructure patterns, where infrastructure components are replaced entirely with each deployment, to ensure consistency and reliability.

3. **Blue-Green Deployments:** Implement blue-green deployments or canary releases to minimize risk during deployments. These practices allow for gradual and controlled releases to specific user segments.

4. **Feature Flags:** Use feature flags or feature toggles to enable or disable specific features in production. This allows for selective feature releases and quick rollbacks if necessary.

5. **Monitoring and Logging:** Establish comprehensive monitoring and logging practices to track application performance, user behavior, and system stability in real-time.

6. **Automated Testing:** Maintain a robust suite of automated tests that cover functional, performance, and security aspects of your application.

7. **Collaboration:** Encourage close collaboration between

development, operations, and other stakeholders to ensure alignment and visibility throughout the CD process.

Continuous Deployment is a cornerstone of modern software delivery, enabling organizations to release software continuously with confidence. By adhering to CD principles and best practices, teams can enhance their software delivery process, reduce risk, and meet the ever-increasing demands of today's fast-paced digital landscape.

C. Continuous Testing: Ensuring Software Quality at Every Stage

Continuous Testing (CT) is a critical practice within the DevOps methodology that focuses on ensuring software quality throughout the entire software development lifecycle (SDLC). Unlike traditional testing approaches that are often conducted as separate and isolated phases, continuous testing integrates testing activities seamlessly into the DevOps pipeline, from code development to deployment and beyond. In this in-depth exploration of Continuous Testing, we'll delve into its principles, benefits, and best practices.

Principles of Continuous Testing:

1. **Early Testing:** Continuous Testing promotes the idea of testing early and often. Instead of waiting for a dedicated

testing phase after development, testing begins as soon as code is written.

2. **Automation:** Automation is at the core of Continuous Testing. Test cases, including unit tests, integration tests, and regression tests, are automated and integrated into the CI/CD pipeline.

3. **Comprehensive Test Coverage:** Continuous Testing aims to cover a wide range of testing types, including functional, non-functional (performance, security), and user acceptance testing. This comprehensive approach helps detect defects and issues across various dimensions.

4. **Feedback Loop:** Continuous Testing provides immediate feedback to developers. Automated tests run on every code commit, allowing developers to address issues quickly, reducing the cost and complexity of fixing defects later in the SDLC.

Benefits of Continuous Testing:

1. **Higher Software Quality:** Continuous Testing ensures that code changes are rigorously tested for defects and regressions before they reach production. This leads to higher software quality and a reduced likelihood of critical issues reaching end-users.

2. **Faster Release Cycles:** By automating testing and making it an integral part of the CI/CD pipeline, Continuous Testing significantly accelerates the software delivery process. This allows organizations to release new features and updates more rapidly.

3. **Improved Collaboration:** Continuous Testing fosters collaboration between development and testing teams. Instead of working in silos, teams collaborate on test case automation, quality metrics, and defect resolution.

4. **Reduced Costs:** Detecting and fixing defects early in the SDLC is more cost-effective than addressing them in later stages or in production. Continuous Testing helps reduce the overall cost of software development and maintenance.

5. **Enhanced User Experience:** By continuously validating application functionality, performance, and security, Continuous Testing helps ensure a positive user experience, leading to higher user satisfaction and retention.

Best Practices for Continuous Testing:

1. **Automate Tests:** Automate as many tests as possible, including unit tests, integration tests, regression tests, and even user acceptance tests. Use testing frameworks and tools suited to your application's technology stack.

2. **Parallel Testing:** Run tests in parallel to reduce testing time. Parallel test execution is particularly important for large and complex applications.

3. **Shift Left Testing:** Begin testing early in the SDLC. Developers should write unit tests and conduct integration testing as part of their coding process.

4. **Test Environment Management:** Maintain consistent and well-managed test environments that closely resemble the production environment. Infrastructure as Code (IaC) can help automate environment provisioning.

5. **Continuous Feedback:** Provide immediate feedback to developers and teams about test results, highlighting failures and issues for rapid resolution.

6. **Test Data Management:** Ensure that test data is managed effectively, and privacy and compliance regulations are followed when handling sensitive data.

7. **Test Reporting and Metrics:** Implement test reporting and metrics to track the effectiveness of testing efforts, identify trends, and continuously improve testing practices.

8. **Security and Performance Testing:** Include security and performance testing in your Continuous Testing strategy to identify vulnerabilities and ensure application scalability.

9. **Cross-Browser and Cross-Platform Testing:** If your application is web-based, conduct cross-browser and cross-platform testing to ensure compatibility across different browsers and devices.

Continuous Testing is an essential practice in DevOps that guarantees software quality at every stage of the SDLC. By embracing Continuous Testing principles and best practices, organizations can deliver high-quality software faster, minimize defects, and provide a seamless user experience.

D. Infrastructure as Code (IaC): Automating Infrastructure Management

Infrastructure as Code (IaC) is a core DevOps practice that transforms the way infrastructure resources are provisioned, configured, and managed. It treats infrastructure in the same way as software code, enabling organizations to automate and standardize their infrastructure operations. In this comprehensive exploration of IaC, we'll delve into its principles, benefits, and best practices.

Principles of Infrastructure as Code:

1. **Declarative Configuration:** IaC uses code (often in the form of scripts or configuration files) to declare the desired state of infrastructure resources. Instead of specifying step-by-step

instructions for provisioning and configuring resources, IaC defines the desired end state, and automation tools take care of the execution.

2. **Version Control:** IaC leverages version control systems like Git to manage infrastructure code. This enables tracking changes, rolling back to previous configurations, and collaborating on infrastructure changes as a team.

3. **Automation:** Automation is at the heart of IaC. Infrastructure provisioning, configuration, and scaling are all automated processes, reducing the need for manual intervention and minimizing human error.

4. **Idempotent Operations:** IaC scripts and templates are designed to be idempotent, meaning that running them multiple times produces the same result as running them once. This ensures consistency and predictability in infrastructure operations.

Benefits of Infrastructure as Code:

1. **Scalability:** IaC makes it easy to scale infrastructure resources up or down as needed, responding to changing workloads and demands without manual intervention.

2. **Consistency:** IaC ensures that infrastructure resources are consistently provisioned and configured across different

environments, reducing configuration drift and minimizing inconsistencies.

3. **Reproducibility:** Infrastructure configurations are defined as code, making it possible to recreate environments and resources accurately and reliably.

4. **Efficiency:** Automating infrastructure operations saves time and resources, reducing the operational overhead and enabling teams to focus on higher-value tasks.

5. **Collaboration:** IaC promotes collaboration among teams by providing a standardized way to manage infrastructure and enabling version-controlled infrastructure code.

6. **Disaster Recovery:** In the event of a failure or disaster, IaC allows for quick and reliable recovery by recreating infrastructure resources based on code definitions.

Best Practices for Infrastructure as Code:

1. **Choose the Right IaC Tool:** Select an IaC tool or framework that aligns with your organization's needs and technology stack. Popular options include Terraform, Ansible, Chef, Puppet, and AWS CloudFormation.

2. **Modularization:** Organize infrastructure code into reusable modules or templates. This promotes code reusability and simplifies maintenance.

3. **Version Control:** Store infrastructure code in a version control system like Git, and follow best practices for branching, merging, and documenting changes.

4. **Testing:** Implement automated testing for your IaC code to catch errors and issues early. This includes syntax checking, linting, and integration testing with real cloud or infrastructure environments.

5. **Parameterization:** Use parameterization to make infrastructure code adaptable to different environments or configurations. This allows you to reuse code for various use cases.

6. **Secrets Management:** Safeguard sensitive information, such as API keys and passwords, using a secure secrets management solution. Avoid hardcoding secrets in IaC code.

7. **Documentation:** Maintain clear and up-to-date documentation for your IaC code and infrastructure configurations. Documentation should include purpose, usage instructions, and dependencies.

8. **Audit and Monitoring:** Implement auditing and monitoring to track changes made to infrastructure resources and configurations. This helps ensure compliance and security.

9. **Collaboration:** Encourage collaboration and communication

between development and operations teams to ensure that IaC code aligns with business requirements and performance expectations.

10. **Continuous Improvement:** Continuously review and refine your IaC code and practices to optimize infrastructure operations and maintain a high level of efficiency.

Infrastructure as Code is a game-changing practice in the DevOps landscape, enabling organizations to automate and standardize infrastructure management. By embracing IaC principles and best practices, teams can achieve greater efficiency, scalability, and consistency in their infrastructure operations, ultimately leading to improved software delivery and operational excellence.

E. Configuration Management: Maintaining Consistency and Compliance

Configuration Management is a fundamental practice within the DevOps framework that focuses on the systematic management of software and infrastructure configurations. It ensures that systems are set up consistently, changes are tracked and controlled, and compliance requirements are met. In this comprehensive exploration of Configuration Management, we'll delve into its principles, benefits, and best practices.

Principles of Configuration Management:

1. **Consistency:** Configuration Management seeks to ensure that all systems and environments are configured consistently. This consistency helps eliminate configuration drift, where systems diverge from their desired states over time.

2. **Automation:** Automation is a key component of Configuration Management. Tools and scripts are used to define and enforce desired configurations across multiple systems and environments.

3. **Version Control:** Configuration Management relies on version control systems to manage and track changes to configuration files and scripts. This enables auditing, rollback, and collaboration.

4. **Auditing and Compliance:** Configuration Management facilitates auditing and compliance efforts by ensuring that systems adhere to regulatory requirements and security standards.

Benefits of Configuration Management:

1. **Consistency:** Configuration Management ensures that systems are set up and configured consistently, reducing the likelihood of configuration-related issues.

2. **Efficiency:** Automation in Configuration Management

streamlines repetitive tasks such as software installations and updates, reducing manual intervention and minimizing errors.

3. **Version Control:** Version control for configuration files and scripts provides visibility into changes and simplifies the process of identifying and resolving configuration-related issues.

4. **Scalability:** Configuration Management enables organizations to scale infrastructure and software configurations easily, responding to changing requirements and workloads.

5. **Security and Compliance:** By enforcing security configurations and compliance standards, Configuration Management helps mitigate security risks and maintain regulatory compliance.

6. **Disaster Recovery:** In the event of system failures or disasters, Configuration Management facilitates quick recovery by providing consistent, documented configuration states.

Best Practices for Configuration Management:

1. **Use a Configuration Management Tool:** Select a Configuration Management tool or framework that suits your organization's needs. Popular choices include Ansible, Chef,

Puppet, and SaltStack.

2. **Infrastructure as Code (IaC):** Integrate Configuration Management into your Infrastructure as Code (IaC) practices. IaC tools like Terraform can automate infrastructure provisioning and configuration.

3. **Centralized Repository:** Maintain a centralized repository for configuration files and scripts, enabling version control, auditing, and collaboration.

4. **Modularization:** Organize configuration code into reusable modules or roles. This promotes code reusability and simplifies maintenance.

5. **Testing:** Implement automated testing of configuration changes to catch errors and issues early. This includes syntax checking, linting, and integration testing.

6. **Parameterization:** Use parameterization to make configuration code adaptable to different environments or configurations. Avoid hardcoding values whenever possible.

7. **Documentation:** Maintain clear and up-to-date documentation for configuration settings and changes. Documentation should include descriptions, dependencies, and usage instructions.

8. **Change Management:** Implement change management

processes to control and document configuration changes. This includes change approvals and rollback plans.

9. **Security Hardening:** Apply security best practices to configuration settings to ensure that systems are resilient to threats and vulnerabilities.

10. **Compliance Checks:** Integrate compliance checks into your Configuration Management processes to ensure that systems meet regulatory and security requirements.

11. **Monitoring and Alerts:** Implement monitoring and alerting for configuration drift. Detect and respond to any deviations from the desired configuration state.

Configuration Management is a cornerstone of reliable and secure IT operations. By embracing Configuration Management principles and best practices, organizations can achieve greater consistency, efficiency, and compliance in their software and infrastructure configurations, ultimately contributing to a more robust and resilient IT environment.

CHAPTER 3

Introduction to DevOps Tools and Technologies

DevOps is a methodology that emphasizes automation, collaboration, and continuous improvement to streamline the software development and deployment process. At its core, DevOps relies on a rich ecosystem of tools and technologies designed to facilitate and enhance various aspects of the development pipeline. From source code management and build automation to containerization and monitoring, these tools play a pivotal role in enabling organizations to achieve their DevOps goals.

In this section, we embark on a journey through the diverse landscape of DevOps tools and technologies. We will explore their functionalities, use cases, and the value they bring to the DevOps process. Whether you are a developer seeking to optimize your coding workflow or an operations professional aiming to enhance deployment and monitoring, understanding these tools is key to mastering the art of DevOps and accelerating your software delivery pipeline. So, let's dive into the world of DevOps tools and technologies and discover how they empower teams to deliver software faster and with greater reliability.

A. Source Code Management (e.g., Git)

Source Code Management (SCM), with Git as one of its most popular implementations, is a fundamental component of DevOps and software development. SCM tools enable teams to efficiently manage, version, collaborate on, and track changes to source code, ensuring that the development process is streamlined, organized, and collaborative. In this in-depth exploration of Source Code Management, we'll focus on Git and its principles, benefits, and best practices.

Principles of Source Code Management with Git:

1. **Version Control:** Git provides version control, allowing developers to track changes made to their code over time. This ensures that previous versions of the code can be retrieved if needed, facilitating collaboration and code history tracking.

2. **Distributed Development:** Git is a distributed version control system (DVCS), meaning that every developer has their own copy of the entire repository. This decentralization enables offline work and collaboration without a centralized server.

3. **Branching and Merging:** Git supports branching and merging, allowing developers to work on separate features or bug fixes in isolated branches. These branches can later be merged into the main codebase, maintaining code stability.

4. **Committing and Staging:** Developers commit their changes

to Git, providing a snapshot of the code at a specific point in time. They can stage specific changes for commit, enabling granular control over what gets saved.

5. **Conflict Resolution:** Git provides tools for resolving conflicts that may arise when multiple developers modify the same code simultaneously. This ensures that code changes are merged harmoniously.

Benefits of Source Code Management with Git:

1. **Version History:** Git's version control capability allows developers to track changes, understand how the code evolved over time, and easily revert to previous states when necessary.

2. **Collaboration:** Git fosters collaboration among development teams by enabling multiple developers to work on different parts of a project concurrently. Branches and pull requests facilitate code review and integration.

3. **Traceability:** Git provides detailed logs and commit messages, making it easier to trace who made specific changes and why they were made. This aids in troubleshooting and code accountability.

4. **Branching Strategy:** Git's branching and merging capabilities enable teams to adopt branching strategies like GitFlow or Feature Branching, which improve code stability

and release management.

5. **Backup and Recovery:** The distributed nature of Git ensures that every developer has a full copy of the repository, acting as a built-in backup mechanism. This safeguards against data loss.

Best Practices for Source Code Management with Git:

1. **Use Descriptive Commit Messages:** Write clear and descriptive commit messages that explain why a change was made and its impact.

2. **Branch Naming Conventions:** Adopt consistent branch naming conventions to make it easier to identify the purpose of each branch.

3. **Frequent Commits:** Commit small, incremental changes frequently rather than large, infrequent commits. This simplifies code review and helps maintain a clean version history.

4. **Code Reviews:** Implement code review processes to ensure code quality and catch issues early. Tools like GitLab, GitHub, and Bitbucket provide features for code review.

5. **.gitignore File:** Use a **.gitignore** file to specify files and directories that should be excluded from version control, such as build artifacts or sensitive data.

6. **Pull Requests:** Encourage the use of pull requests or merge requests for code integration. They provide a controlled process for code review and collaboration.

7. **Git Hooks:** Leverage Git hooks to automate tasks like running tests or formatting code before commits or pushes.

8. **Documentation:** Maintain clear and up-to-date documentation, including README files and project wikis, to help team members understand project structure and processes.

9. **Git Tags:** Use Git tags to mark specific points in your codebase, such as releases or milestones, for easy reference.

10. **Security:** Implement security best practices, such as requiring two-factor authentication for repositories and using access controls to restrict access to sensitive code.

Git is a versatile and widely adopted source code management tool that plays a crucial role in modern software development and DevOps practices. By adhering to Git's principles and best practices, development teams can collaborate effectively, maintain code quality, and ensure the reliability and traceability of their codebase.

B. Build Tools in DevOps: Automating the Software Build Process with Jenkins

Build tools are essential components of the DevOps toolkit, responsible for automating the process of compiling, assembling, and packaging source code into executable software artifacts. One of the most popular and versatile build tools in the DevOps landscape is Jenkins. In this in-depth exploration of build tools, with a focus on Jenkins, we'll delve into their principles, benefits, and best practices.

Principles of Build Tools:

1. **Automation:** Build tools automate the build process, eliminating the need for manual compilation and packaging of source code. This automation ensures consistency and repeatability.

2. **Integration:** Build tools integrate seamlessly into the DevOps pipeline, allowing developers to trigger builds automatically when code changes are committed. Integration with version control systems is a key feature.

3. **Artifact Generation:** Build tools generate executable artifacts, such as binaries, libraries, or container images, from the source code. These artifacts can then be deployed to various environments.

4. **Testing:** Build tools can incorporate automated testing into the

build process, running unit tests, integration tests, and other checks to ensure the quality and reliability of the software.

Benefits of Build Tools, including Jenkins:

1. **Consistency:** Build tools ensure that builds are executed consistently across different environments, reducing the risk of configuration-related issues.

2. **Automation:** Automated builds save time and reduce human error. Developers can focus on coding while the build process is handled by the tool.

3. **Integration:** Build tools integrate with other DevOps tools and processes, enabling continuous integration and delivery (CI/CD) pipelines.

4. **Parallelization:** Many build tools, including Jenkins, support parallel builds, allowing multiple tasks to run concurrently, further speeding up the build process.

5. **Extensibility:** Jenkins, in particular, is highly extensible with a vast ecosystem of plugins. Custom build workflows and integrations can be created to suit specific project needs.

Jenkins as a Build Tool:

Jenkins is an open-source automation server that excels in automating the build, test, and deployment phases of software development. It offers a range of features that make it a preferred choice for many DevOps teams:

1. **Freestyle and Pipeline Jobs:** Jenkins supports both freestyle and pipeline jobs. Freestyle jobs are easy to set up and configure, while pipeline jobs provide more flexibility and scalability, allowing you to define complex build workflows as code.

2. **Vast Plugin Ecosystem:** Jenkins boasts a vast plugin ecosystem, with thousands of plugins available to extend its functionality. You can find plugins for integrating with version control systems, build tools, deployment platforms, and more.

3. **Distributed Builds:** Jenkins can distribute build tasks across multiple agents, enabling parallel builds and improving build performance.

4. **Customization:** Jenkins provides extensive configuration options, allowing you to tailor your build environment to the specific needs of your project.

5. **Integration:** Jenkins integrates seamlessly with popular version control systems like Git and SVN, as well as with containerization technologies like Docker and Kubernetes.

Best Practices for Using Build Tools, including Jenkins:

1. **Automate Everything:** Automate as much of the build process as possible, including code compilation, testing, and artifact generation.

2. **Version Control:** Store build configurations as code in version control to maintain a history of changes and facilitate collaboration.

3. **Dependency Management:** Keep track of project dependencies, and use dependency management tools like Maven or Gradle to manage them.

4. **Build Artifacts:** Ensure that build artifacts are properly versioned and stored in a central repository for traceability and reproducibility.

5. **Testing:** Incorporate automated testing into the build process to catch issues early and ensure software quality.

6. **Parallel Builds:** Utilize parallelization capabilities to speed up builds, especially for large projects.

7. **Continuous Integration:** Integrate build tools into a CI/CD pipeline for automated testing and deployment.

8. **Monitoring:** Implement monitoring and alerting for build jobs to quickly identify and address build failures or performance

issues.

Build tools like Jenkins are pivotal in DevOps, automating critical aspects of software development and delivery. By following best practices and integrating build tools effectively into your DevOps workflows, you can accelerate the software development process, improve code quality, and streamline the path to production deployment.

C. Containerization with Docker: Streamlining Application Deployment and Management

Containerization is a transformative technology in the DevOps and software development landscape, revolutionizing the way applications are packaged, deployed, and managed. Docker, one of the most popular containerization platforms, has played a central role in this evolution. In this comprehensive exploration of containerization, with a focus on Docker, we will delve into its principles, benefits, and best practices.

Principles of Containerization:

1. **Lightweight Isolation:** Containers are lightweight and isolated environments that encapsulate an application and its dependencies, ensuring consistency across different environments.

2. **Portability:** Containers are highly portable. Once created, a

container can run consistently on any system that supports containerization, regardless of the underlying infrastructure.

3. **Resource Efficiency:** Containers share the host operating system's kernel, which results in efficient resource utilization and minimal overhead compared to traditional virtualization.

4. **Immutable Infrastructure:** Containers are designed to be immutable, meaning they are never modified once created. To make changes, a new container image is created, promoting consistency and predictability.

Benefits of Containerization with Docker:

1. **Consistency:** Containers ensure that applications run consistently across different environments, reducing the "it works on my machine" problem.

2. **Portability:** Docker containers can be run on developer laptops, test servers, and production environments, providing a consistent runtime environment throughout the software development lifecycle.

3. **Resource Efficiency:** Containers are lightweight and efficient, allowing for high-density deployments on a single host.

4. **Versioning and Rollback:** Docker images are versioned, making it easy to roll back to previous versions of an

application if issues arise.

5. **Isolation:** Containers provide process and file system isolation, ensuring that applications do not interfere with each other.

Docker as a Containerization Platform:

Docker has become synonymous with containerization, thanks to its user-friendly interface, robust tooling, and extensive ecosystem. Key features and components of Docker include:

1. **Docker Engine:** The core runtime that allows you to create, run, and manage containers. It includes a container daemon, a REST API, and a command-line interface (CLI).

2. **Docker Hub:** A cloud-based registry service where you can find and share container images. Docker Hub hosts millions of publicly available images and enables you to publish your own.

3. **Docker Compose:** A tool for defining and running multi-container applications. Docker Compose uses YAML files to define application services, networks, and volumes.

4. **Docker Swarm:** Docker's native orchestration and clustering solution, which allows you to manage and scale containers across multiple hosts.

5. **Kubernetes Integration:** Docker containers can be orchestrated and managed using Kubernetes, making Docker a key component of many Kubernetes-based deployments.

Best Practices for Containerization with Docker:

1. **Use Official Images:** Whenever possible, use official Docker images from trusted sources like Docker Hub or the official repository for the base image.

2. **Keep Containers Single-Purpose:** Follow the principle of "one service per container" to keep containers lightweight and focused on specific tasks.

3. **Version Containers:** Tag your container images with version numbers or commit hashes for traceability and easy rollback.

4. **Dockerfile Best Practices:** Write efficient and secure Dockerfiles. Use multi-stage builds to minimize image size, and avoid including unnecessary packages or secrets.

5. **Container Security:** Regularly scan container images for vulnerabilities using tools like Docker Security Scanning or third-party solutions.

6. **Resource Limits:** Define resource limits (CPU and memory) for containers to ensure fair resource allocation and prevent resource contention.

7. **Logging and Monitoring:** Implement logging and monitoring for containers to track their performance and troubleshoot issues.

8. **Backup and Recovery:** Develop backup and recovery strategies for containerized applications, including data volumes.

9. **Immutable Infrastructure:** Embrace the concept of immutable infrastructure by rebuilding and redeploying containers rather than making changes in-place.

Containerization with Docker has reshaped how applications are developed, deployed, and managed in the DevOps world. By adhering to best practices and leveraging Docker's capabilities effectively, organizations can achieve greater consistency, portability, and resource efficiency in their software delivery pipeline.

D. Orchestration with Kubernetes: Scaling, Automating, and Managing Containerized Applications

Orchestration plays a pivotal role in the world of DevOps and containerization, enabling organizations to efficiently deploy, manage, and scale containerized applications. Kubernetes, often abbreviated as K8s, is the industry-standard orchestration platform known for its robust features and ecosystem. In this comprehensive exploration of orchestration, with a focus on Kubernetes, we'll delve into its principles, benefits, and best practices.

Principles of Orchestration:

1. **Resource Management:** Orchestration platforms like Kubernetes manage the allocation of computing resources (CPU, memory, storage) to containerized applications, ensuring optimal utilization.

2. **Scaling:** Orchestration platforms facilitate horizontal scaling, allowing applications to automatically adjust the number of running containers based on demand.

3. **High Availability:** Orchestration ensures that applications remain highly available by automatically distributing containers across multiple nodes and recovering from failures.

4. **Service Discovery:** Orchestration platforms provide service discovery and load balancing capabilities, enabling containers to find and communicate with each other.

Benefits of Orchestration with Kubernetes:

1. **Efficiency:** Kubernetes automates many aspects of application management, reducing the manual effort required for deployment, scaling, and maintenance.

2. **Scalability:** Kubernetes can automatically scale applications up or down based on resource utilization or custom-defined metrics, ensuring applications can handle varying workloads.

3. **High Availability:** Kubernetes manages container placement and resiliency, minimizing downtime and service interruptions.

4. **Portability:** Kubernetes abstracts away the underlying infrastructure, making applications highly portable and allowing them to run consistently across different environments.

5. **Service Discovery and Load Balancing:** Kubernetes provides built-in service discovery and load balancing, simplifying communication between containers and ensuring even traffic distribution.

Kubernetes as an Orchestration Platform:

Kubernetes is an open-source container orchestration platform that has become the de facto standard for container management and orchestration. It offers several key components and features:

1. **Nodes:** Kubernetes clusters consist of nodes (servers) that run containers. Nodes can be physical servers or virtual machines.

2. **Pods:** Pods are the smallest deployable units in Kubernetes and can contain one or more containers. Containers within the

same pod share the same network namespace and storage volumes.

3. **Services:** Kubernetes services provide a stable network endpoint for accessing a set of pods, enabling load balancing and service discovery.

4. **ReplicaSets:** ReplicaSets ensure a specified number of identical pod replicas are running, providing fault tolerance and scalability.

5. **Deployments:** Deployments manage updates to applications by controlling the rollout of new replicas and monitoring the health of existing ones.

6. **ConfigMaps and Secrets:** ConfigMaps store configuration data as key-value pairs, while Secrets store sensitive information, such as passwords and API keys.

7. **Namespaces:** Namespaces provide a way to logically partition a Kubernetes cluster, allowing multiple teams or applications to coexist within the same cluster.

Best Practices for Orchestration with Kubernetes:

1. **Infrastructure as Code (IaC):** Use Infrastructure as Code (IaC) principles and tools like Terraform or Ansible to provision and manage Kubernetes clusters.

2. **Container Best Practices:** Follow container best practices, such as keeping containers lightweight and adhering to the "one service per container" principle.

3. **Resource Limits and Requests:** Define resource limits and requests for containers to ensure fair resource allocation and prevent resource contention.

4. **High Availability:** Design for high availability by distributing workloads across multiple nodes and using multi-zone deployments.

5. **Horizontal Pod Autoscaling:** Configure Horizontal Pod Autoscaling to automatically adjust the number of pod replicas based on resource utilization.

6. **Health Checks:** Implement readiness and liveness probes to ensure that applications are healthy and available for traffic.

7. **Logging and Monitoring:** Set up logging and monitoring solutions like Prometheus and Grafana to gain visibility into the performance of your Kubernetes clusters and applications.

8. **Security:** Implement security best practices, such as RBAC (Role-Based Access Control) and network policies, to secure your Kubernetes environment.

9. **Backup and Disaster Recovery:** Develop backup and disaster recovery strategies for both application data and

Kubernetes configuration.

10. **Continuous Deployment:** Integrate Kubernetes into your CI/CD pipeline for automated application deployment and updates.

Kubernetes is a powerful orchestration platform that has revolutionized how organizations manage and scale containerized applications. By following best practices and leveraging Kubernetes effectively, teams can achieve greater efficiency, scalability, and reliability in their container orchestration efforts, ultimately delivering more resilient and responsive applications to users.

E. Monitoring and Logging Tools in DevOps: Gaining Insights for Optimal Performance

Monitoring and logging tools are indispensable components of the DevOps toolkit, providing insights into the health, performance, and behavior of applications and infrastructure. These tools enable organizations to proactively identify and address issues, troubleshoot problems, and optimize system performance. In this comprehensive exploration of monitoring and logging tools, we'll delve into their principles, benefits, and best practices.

Principles of Monitoring and Logging:

1. **Observability:** Monitoring and logging together contribute to the concept of observability, which encompasses the ability to understand and diagnose system behavior by collecting and analyzing relevant data.

2. **Metrics and Events:** Monitoring tools gather metrics, which are quantitative measurements of system performance, while logging tools record events and activities in text-based logs for later analysis.

3. **Alerting:** Monitoring tools often include alerting capabilities that notify teams when predefined thresholds or conditions are met, allowing for timely responses to issues.

Benefits of Monitoring and Logging:

1. **Proactive Issue Detection:** Monitoring tools provide real-time visibility into system performance, enabling teams to identify and address issues before they impact users.

2. **Root Cause Analysis:** Logging tools record detailed information about system events, making it easier to pinpoint the root causes of problems and troubleshoot issues effectively.

3. **Performance Optimization:** By analyzing metrics and logs, organizations can fine-tune their systems for optimal

performance and resource utilization.

4. **Capacity Planning:** Monitoring data helps organizations plan for resource scaling and capacity adjustments based on usage trends and patterns.

5. **Compliance and Auditing:** Logging is crucial for compliance with regulatory requirements and security audits, as it provides a detailed record of system activities.

Monitoring Tools:

1. **Prometheus:** An open-source monitoring and alerting toolkit that excels at collecting and storing time-series data. It is highly extensible and integrates well with Grafana for visualization.

2. **Datadog:** A cloud-based monitoring and analytics platform that offers real-time insights into application and infrastructure performance, along with advanced alerting and visualization features.

3. **New Relic:** A SaaS-based application performance monitoring (APM) tool that provides end-to-end visibility into application performance and user experience.

4. **Nagios:** An open-source monitoring system known for its flexibility and extensibility, with a wide range of plugins and integrations.

Logging Tools:

1. **Elasticsearch, Logstash, and Kibana (ELK Stack):** An open-source stack for searching, analyzing, and visualizing log data. Elasticsearch is used for storage and search, Logstash for data processing, and Kibana for visualization.

2. **Splunk:** A widely-used platform for collecting, indexing, and analyzing machine-generated data, including logs, metrics, and events.

3. **Graylog:** An open-source log management platform that allows organizations to collect, index, and analyze log data.

Best Practices for Monitoring and Logging:

1. **Define Key Metrics:** Identify the most critical metrics and logs to monitor based on the specific needs and goals of your application and infrastructure.

2. **Granularity:** Choose an appropriate level of granularity for your monitoring and logging data to strike a balance between detail and resource usage.

3. **Alerting Thresholds:** Set meaningful alerting thresholds to avoid false alarms and ensure that alerts are actionable.

4. **Distributed Tracing:** Implement distributed tracing tools like OpenTelemetry or Zipkin to gain insights into the performance

of microservices architectures.

5. **Log Retention and Rotation:** Define log retention and rotation policies to manage log data efficiently, comply with regulations, and optimize storage costs.

6. **Data Security:** Secure access to monitoring and logging data by implementing authentication, authorization, and encryption mechanisms.

7. **Automated Remediation:** Integrate monitoring tools with automation frameworks to trigger automated responses to common issues.

8. **Documentation:** Document the architecture and configuration of your monitoring and logging tools to facilitate troubleshooting and onboarding of new team members.

Monitoring and logging are essential practices in DevOps, providing the visibility and insights needed to maintain the reliability and performance of modern applications and infrastructure. By selecting the right tools, defining clear monitoring and logging strategies, and adhering to best practices, organizations can proactively manage their systems, troubleshoot issues efficiently, and continuously optimize their operations.

F. Collaboration Tools in DevOps: Enhancing Communication and Efficiency

Collaboration tools are a cornerstone of DevOps, facilitating communication, coordination, and teamwork among development, operations, and other cross-functional teams. These tools streamline collaboration by providing a centralized platform for sharing information, tracking work, and managing projects. In this comprehensive exploration of collaboration tools in DevOps, we'll delve into their principles, benefits, and best practices, with a focus on two popular tools: Slack and Jira.

Principles of Collaboration Tools:

1. **Centralization:** Collaboration tools centralize communication and information sharing, reducing the need for scattered emails, chats, and documents.

2. **Real-Time Communication:** Many collaboration tools offer real-time messaging and chat features, enabling instant communication and rapid decision-making.

3. **Work Tracking:** Collaboration tools often include features for tracking tasks, projects, and work items, providing visibility into progress and priorities.

Benefits of Collaboration Tools:

1. **Improved Communication:** Collaboration tools enhance

communication by providing channels and chat threads for discussions, announcements, and updates.

2. **Enhanced Transparency:** Collaboration tools promote transparency by making project information and updates accessible to all team members.

3. **Streamlined Workflow:** With work tracking and project management features, collaboration tools help teams organize and prioritize tasks, reducing bottlenecks and delays.

4. **Reduced Email Overload:** Collaboration tools reduce the reliance on email for internal communication, leading to more focused and efficient use of email for external communication.

5. **Integration Capabilities:** Many collaboration tools integrate with other DevOps tools, such as version control systems and continuous integration/continuous deployment (CI/CD) pipelines, streamlining workflows.

Collaboration Tools:

1. **Slack:** A widely-used team messaging and collaboration platform that offers channels for organized discussions, direct messaging, file sharing, and integrations with various third-party tools.

2. **Jira:** A popular project and issue tracking tool developed by Atlassian. Jira is highly customizable and can be adapted for

various DevOps use cases, including agile software development and IT service management.

Best Practices for Collaboration Tools:

1. **Create Structured Channels:** In Slack, organize discussions into channels based on projects, teams, or topics to keep conversations focused and searchable.

2. **Use Threaded Conversations:** Encourage the use of threaded conversations in Slack to keep discussions organized and prevent message overload in channels.

3. **Integrate with DevOps Tools:** Integrate collaboration tools with other DevOps tools, such as version control systems and CI/CD pipelines, to receive automated notifications and updates.

4. **Set Notification Preferences:** Configure notification settings to avoid alert fatigue while ensuring you receive important updates promptly.

5. **Customize Workflows:** In Jira, tailor workflows and issue types to match your team's specific processes and needs.

6. **Prioritize and Assign Work:** Use collaboration tools to prioritize tasks, assign work to team members, and track progress toward milestones.

7. **Document Decisions:** In collaboration tools like Slack, document important decisions and discussions in dedicated channels or threads for future reference.

8. **Security and Access Controls:** Implement security best practices by defining access controls and permissions to protect sensitive information.

9. **Training and Onboarding:** Provide training and onboarding resources to help team members effectively use collaboration tools and follow best practices.

10. **Regular Cleanup:** Periodically review and archive channels, threads, or issues that are no longer relevant to maintain a clutter-free workspace.

Collaboration tools like Slack and Jira are essential enablers of efficient communication and teamwork in DevOps. By adopting these tools and adhering to best practices, organizations can streamline their workflows, enhance transparency, and foster a culture of collaboration that contributes to the success of their DevOps initiatives.

CHAPTER 4

Introduction to Automation in DevOps

Automation is the beating heart of DevOps, powering its ability to streamline processes, enhance efficiency, and deliver software at unprecedented speeds. At its core, DevOps is all about removing bottlenecks, reducing manual intervention, and automating repetitive tasks across the software development and delivery lifecycle. In this section, we embark on a journey through the world of automation in DevOps, exploring its fundamental principles, the tools and technologies that make it possible, and the profound impact it has on accelerating the pace of software development while maintaining reliability and quality. Automation is the secret sauce that empowers DevOps teams to achieve more, faster, and with higher precision, and we're about to dive deep into how it works and why it matters.

A. Scripting and Automation Languages in DevOps: Empowering Efficiency and Scalability

Scripting and automation languages are the building blocks of DevOps, enabling organizations to automate a wide range of tasks and processes across the software development and delivery pipeline. These languages play a pivotal role in reducing manual effort, increasing efficiency, and ensuring consistency in DevOps workflows. In this comprehensive exploration of scripting and automation languages, we'll delve into their principles, benefits, and best practices.

Principles of Scripting and Automation Languages:

1. **Abstraction:** Scripting languages provide a higher-level abstraction over manual operations, allowing developers and operators to describe tasks in a more concise and human-readable manner.

2. **Repeatability:** Automation languages enable the creation of scripts and code that can be reused across different environments, ensuring consistent outcomes.

3. **Extensibility:** Scripting languages often come with libraries and modules that extend their functionality, enabling users to build custom automation solutions.

4. **Integration:** Automation languages can interface with various tools, APIs, and services, facilitating the integration of disparate systems and processes.

Benefits of Scripting and Automation Languages:

1. **Efficiency:** Scripting and automation languages streamline repetitive and time-consuming tasks, reducing manual

intervention and the risk of errors.

2. **Scalability:** Automation languages enable the automation of tasks at scale, making it feasible to manage large and complex infrastructures efficiently.

3. **Consistency:** Automation ensures that tasks are executed consistently, eliminating variability and reducing the likelihood of configuration drift.

4. **Resource Optimization:** Automated processes can be scheduled to run during off-peak hours, optimizing resource utilization and reducing operational costs.

5. **Auditability:** Scripts and automation code provide a traceable record of actions taken, enhancing accountability and troubleshooting.

Popular Scripting and Automation Languages:

1. **Python:** Widely recognized for its simplicity and readability, Python is a versatile scripting language used extensively in DevOps for tasks ranging from automation to web development.

2. **Bash:** The Bourne Again Shell (Bash) is a Unix shell scripting language commonly used for system administration and automation on Unix-like operating systems.

3. **PowerShell:** Developed by Microsoft, PowerShell is a powerful automation framework and scripting language for Windows environments.

4. **Ruby:** Known for its elegant syntax, Ruby is used in automation and configuration management tools like Chef and Puppet.

5. **JavaScript:** JavaScript, often associated with web development, is also used for automation tasks through runtime environments like Node.js.

Best Practices for Scripting and Automation Languages:

1. **Code Modularity:** Break automation code into reusable functions or modules to promote code maintainability and reusability.

2. **Error Handling:** Implement robust error handling to gracefully manage unexpected conditions and failures.

3. **Documentation:** Include clear comments and documentation within scripts to aid in understanding and troubleshooting.

4. **Version Control:** Store automation code in version control systems like Git to track changes, collaborate, and maintain a history of modifications.

5. **Testing:** Write tests for automation code to verify its

correctness and reliability.

6. **Security:** Implement security best practices, such as securely storing credentials and validating user inputs.

7. **Parameterization:** Parameterize scripts to make them configurable for different environments and use cases.

8. **Monitoring and Logging:** Incorporate logging and monitoring into scripts to track their execution and performance.

9. **Code Review:** Perform code reviews to ensure the quality and adherence to best practices in automation code.

Scripting and automation languages are the backbone of DevOps, empowering teams to achieve more with less effort and greater consistency. By mastering these languages and following best practices, organizations can build robust automation solutions that accelerate software delivery, reduce operational overhead, and enhance the overall quality and reliability of their systems.

B. Workflow Automation in DevOps: Streamlining Processes for Efficiency and Consistency

Workflow automation is a cornerstone of DevOps, playing a pivotal role in optimizing and orchestrating the various stages of the software development and delivery lifecycle. This automation empowers organizations to streamline their processes, reduce manual intervention, and ensure greater consistency and reliability in their workflows. In this comprehensive exploration of workflow automation in DevOps, we'll delve into its principles, benefits, and best practices.

Principles of Workflow Automation:

1. **Orchestration:** Workflow automation involves orchestrating a series of tasks and actions, ensuring they are executed in a coordinated and efficient manner.

2. **Integration:** Automation tools and platforms integrate with various systems, tools, and services, enabling the seamless flow of data and actions across the DevOps pipeline.

3. **Event-Driven:** Workflow automation can be triggered by specific events or conditions, such as code commits, test results, or infrastructure changes.

4. **Scalability:** Automated workflows can handle tasks at scale, adapting to the needs of growing and dynamic environments.

Benefits of Workflow Automation:

1. **Efficiency:** Workflow automation reduces the time and effort required to perform repetitive and manual tasks, boosting overall efficiency.

2. **Consistency:** Automated workflows ensure that tasks are executed consistently, reducing the risk of human error and configuration drift.

3. **Speed:** Automation accelerates processes, enabling organizations to deliver software and updates more rapidly to meet customer demands.

4. **Resource Optimization:** Automated workflows can be scheduled to run during off-peak hours, optimizing resource utilization and reducing operational costs.

5. **Traceability:** Automated workflows provide a clear audit trail, allowing organizations to track and monitor the progress and outcomes of tasks.

Components of Workflow Automation in DevOps:

1. **Automation Tools:** DevOps teams utilize a variety of automation tools and platforms to build, manage, and execute automated workflows. These tools include Jenkins, Ansible, Puppet, Chef, and more.

2. **Integration:** Workflow automation tools often integrate with other DevOps tools and services, such as version control systems, container orchestration platforms, and monitoring solutions.

3. **Scripting and Code:** Custom scripts and code snippets are

used to define and configure automated tasks and actions within workflows.

4. **Orchestration:** Orchestration engines, like Kubernetes for container orchestration or workflow management platforms like Apache Airflow, are used to coordinate and schedule tasks.

Best Practices for Workflow Automation:

1. **Define Clear Objectives:** Clearly define the objectives and expected outcomes of automated workflows to ensure alignment with business goals.

2. **Modular Design:** Break workflows into modular and reusable components to promote flexibility and maintainability.

3. **Error Handling:** Implement robust error-handling mechanisms to gracefully manage exceptions and failures.

4. **Testing:** Rigorously test automated workflows to validate their correctness and reliability.

5. **Documentation:** Document workflows comprehensively, including their dependencies, inputs, outputs, and any required configurations.

6. **Security:** Implement security best practices, such as secure credential management, to protect sensitive information.

7. **Monitoring and Logging:** Incorporate monitoring and logging into workflows to track their execution and performance.

8. **Version Control:** Store workflow definitions and associated code in version control systems to track changes and enable collaboration.

9. **Continuous Improvement:** Regularly review and optimize automated workflows to identify opportunities for improvement.

Workflow automation is a fundamental practice in DevOps, enabling organizations to streamline their processes, reduce operational overhead, and accelerate the delivery of software and updates. By adhering to best practices and leveraging automation tools effectively, teams can achieve greater efficiency, consistency, and agility in their DevOps practices, ultimately delivering higher-quality software to their users.

C. Automated Testing in DevOps: Accelerating Quality Assurance and Continuous Delivery

Automated testing is a linchpin of DevOps, revolutionizing the way software is validated and ensuring the quality and reliability of applications in an agile and continuous delivery environment. This practice involves the use of automated scripts and tools to execute test cases, validate software functionality, and uncover defects throughout the software development lifecycle. In this comprehensive exploration of automated testing in DevOps, we'll delve into its principles, benefits, and best practices.

Principles of Automated Testing:

1. **Repeatability:** Automated tests can be executed consistently and repeatedly, ensuring that software behaves consistently across different environments and configurations.

2. **Efficiency:** Automated tests are significantly faster than manual testing, enabling organizations to perform testing more frequently and earlier in the development process.

3. **Regression Testing:** Automated tests are invaluable for regression testing, allowing teams to quickly detect and address issues introduced by code changes.

4. **Scalability:** Automated testing can be scaled to handle a wide range of test cases, making it suitable for large and complex applications.

Benefits of Automated Testing:

1. **Speed:** Automated tests can be run quickly and frequently, enabling rapid feedback on code changes and reducing time-to-market.

2. **Accuracy:** Automated tests eliminate human errors associated with manual testing, leading to more accurate and consistent results.

3. **Consistency:** Automated tests ensure that test cases are executed consistently, reducing the risk of false positives or false negatives.

4. **Continuous Integration:** Automated tests are seamlessly integrated into the continuous integration/continuous deployment (CI/CD) pipeline, allowing for automated validation of code changes.

5. **Resource Efficiency:** Automated testing reduces the need for manual testers, freeing up resources for more creative and exploratory testing.

Types of Automated Testing:

1. **Unit Testing:** Focuses on testing individual components or functions in isolation to ensure they work as expected.

2. **Integration Testing:** Verifies that different components or modules work together correctly as part of a larger system.

3. **Functional Testing:** Tests the functionality of the application against its specifications, ensuring it meets user requirements.

4. **Regression Testing:** Checks whether new code changes have

introduced defects or regressions in existing functionality.

5. **Performance Testing:** Evaluates the application's performance and scalability under various load conditions.

6. **Security Testing:** Identifies security vulnerabilities and weaknesses in the application's code and configuration.

Automated Testing Tools:

1. **Selenium:** A popular open-source tool for automating web browsers, widely used for functional and regression testing of web applications.

2. **JUnit/TestNG:** Java-based testing frameworks for writing and running unit and integration tests in Java applications.

3. **PyTest:** A Python testing framework known for its simplicity and extensibility, suitable for various testing types.

4. **Jenkins:** An automation server that can be used to automate the execution of tests as part of a CI/CD pipeline.

5. **Postman:** A popular tool for automating and testing APIs, including functional and load testing.

Best Practices for Automated Testing:

1. **Early Integration:** Integrate automated tests into the development process from the beginning, running them

frequently and consistently.

2. **Test Coverage:** Aim for comprehensive test coverage to ensure that critical paths and functionality are thoroughly tested.

3. **Continuous Integration:** Incorporate automated tests into the CI/CD pipeline to validate code changes automatically.

4. **Parameterization:** Parameterize test data and configurations to enable the reuse of test cases with different inputs.

5. **Test Data Management:** Manage and maintain test data separately to ensure data integrity and repeatability of tests.

6. **Test Reporting:** Implement reporting mechanisms that provide clear and actionable feedback on test results.

7. **Maintenance:** Regularly review and update automated tests to keep them aligned with evolving code and requirements.

8. **Parallel Testing:** Use parallel execution of tests to save time and speed up test cycles.

Automated testing is a pivotal practice in DevOps, enabling organizations to deliver high-quality software with speed and confidence. By adopting automated testing and following best practices, DevOps teams can achieve greater efficiency, reduce the risk of defects, and accelerate the delivery of software while maintaining the highest level of quality and reliability.

D. Deployment Automation in DevOps: Efficient, Consistent, and Reliable Software Delivery

Deployment automation is a fundamental practice in DevOps that focuses on automating the process of deploying applications and infrastructure changes to production and other environments. It plays a pivotal role in achieving faster and more reliable software delivery while minimizing manual intervention and human errors. In this comprehensive exploration of deployment automation in DevOps, we'll delve into its principles, benefits, and best practices.

Principles of Deployment Automation:

1. **Consistency:** Automated deployments ensure that each release is deployed consistently across different environments, reducing the risk of configuration drift and errors.

2. **Repeatability:** Deployment automation enables the repeatable and predictable deployment of code changes, eliminating variations between deployments.

3. **Speed:** Automated deployments significantly reduce deployment times, enabling organizations to release software more frequently and respond quickly to customer needs.

4. **Rollback Capability:** Automated deployments often include rollback mechanisms, allowing teams to quickly revert to a previous version in case of issues.

Benefits of Deployment Automation:

1. **Faster Release Cycles:** Deployment automation accelerates the release process, allowing organizations to deliver new features and updates to users more frequently.

2. **Reduced Error Rate:** Automated deployments minimize human errors, leading to more reliable and stable releases.

3. **Lower Operational Costs:** Automation reduces the need for manual intervention and the associated operational overhead.

4. **Improved Collaboration:** Deployment automation encourages collaboration between development, operations, and other teams, fostering a culture of shared responsibility.

5. **Enhanced Scalability:** Automated deployments can easily scale to accommodate the needs of growing and dynamic environments.

Deployment Automation Tools:

1. **Jenkins:** An open-source automation server that supports continuous integration and deployment, allowing for the automation of various deployment tasks.

2. **Ansible:** An automation tool that simplifies configuration management and application deployment through declarative playbooks.

3. **Docker:** A containerization platform that enables consistent and portable application deployments across different environments.

4. **Kubernetes:** An orchestration platform for containerized applications that automates deployment, scaling, and management.

5. **AWS CodeDeploy:** A service that automates code deployments to AWS instances, supporting a variety of application types and environments.

Best Practices for Deployment Automation:

1. **Infrastructure as Code (IaC):** Use IaC principles and tools to define infrastructure configurations in code, allowing for consistent and automated provisioning.

2. **Environment Parity:** Ensure that development, testing, and production environments are as similar as possible to avoid surprises during deployment.

3. **Continuous Integration:** Integrate deployment automation into the continuous integration pipeline to promote the automated testing and deployment of code changes.

4. **Blue-Green Deployments:** Implement blue-green deployments to minimize downtime and risk during releases by routing traffic to the new version gradually.

5. **Automated Testing:** Include automated testing as part of the deployment process to catch issues early and ensure the correctness of deployments.

6. **Rollback Strategy:** Develop a rollback strategy and automate the process to quickly revert to a previous version if issues arise.

7. **Monitoring and Alerts:** Implement monitoring and alerting solutions to detect and respond to issues in real-time during and after deployment.

8. **Version Control:** Store deployment scripts and configurations in version control systems to track changes and enable collaboration.

9. **Documentation:** Maintain comprehensive documentation for deployment processes, configurations, and procedures.

10. **Security:** Implement security best practices, such as secure credential management and vulnerability scanning, to protect deployments.

Deployment automation is a cornerstone of DevOps, enabling organizations to release software efficiently, reliably, and with confidence. By embracing deployment automation and adhering to best practices, DevOps teams can minimize deployment-related risks, accelerate the delivery of software, and ensure that each release meets the highest quality and performance standards.

E. Monitoring and Alerting Automation in DevOps: Proactive Insights for Continuous Improvement

Monitoring and alerting automation are critical components of a robust DevOps strategy, providing real-time visibility into the health and performance of applications and infrastructure. These practices enable organizations to detect issues, troubleshoot problems, and optimize system performance efficiently. In this comprehensive exploration of monitoring and alerting automation in DevOps, we'll delve into their principles, benefits, and best practices.

Principles of Monitoring and Alerting Automation:

1. **Continuous Visibility:** Monitoring automation provides continuous visibility into the behavior of applications and infrastructure, allowing teams to react promptly to changes and anomalies.

2. **Proactive Insights:** Alerting automation notifies teams about predefined thresholds or conditions, enabling them to take

proactive actions before issues affect users.

3. **Data-Driven Decision-Making:** Monitoring automation generates data and metrics that inform decision-making, helping teams optimize performance and resource utilization.

4. **Scalability:** Automated monitoring and alerting solutions can scale to accommodate the needs of growing and dynamic environments.

Benefits of Monitoring and Alerting Automation:

1. **Proactive Issue Detection:** Monitoring automation detects anomalies and issues in real-time, allowing teams to address them before they impact users.

2. **Efficient Troubleshooting:** Automated alerting provides context and information needed for efficient troubleshooting, reducing downtime and mean-time-to-resolution (MTTR).

3. **Optimized Performance:** Continuous monitoring and alerting help organizations fine-tune their systems for optimal performance and resource utilization.

4. **Resource Management:** Monitoring and alerting automation assist in resource management and capacity planning based on usage trends and patterns.

5. **Compliance and Security:** Automated monitoring aids in

compliance with regulatory requirements and security audits by providing a detailed record of system activities.

Components of Monitoring and Alerting Automation:

1. **Monitoring Tools:** DevOps teams use monitoring tools to collect and store performance data, including metrics, logs, and events. Common tools include Prometheus, Datadog, and New Relic.

2. **Alerting Systems:** Alerting systems, often integrated with monitoring tools, allow teams to define and manage alerting rules and thresholds. Examples include Prometheus Alertmanager and Nagios.

3. **Log Management:** Log management solutions store and analyze log data, providing insights into application and system behavior. ELK Stack (Elasticsearch, Logstash, Kibana) and Splunk are popular choices.

Best Practices for Monitoring and Alerting Automation:

1. **Define Key Metrics:** Identify and monitor the most critical metrics and events based on specific objectives and user expectations.

2. **Thresholds and Alerts:** Set meaningful thresholds and alerts to avoid alert fatigue and ensure that alerts are actionable.

3. **Automation Rules:** Implement automated actions and responses for common alerts to reduce manual intervention and response times.

4. **Integration:** Integrate monitoring and alerting solutions with other DevOps tools, such as version control systems and CI/CD pipelines, for seamless workflows.

5. **Distributed Tracing:** Implement distributed tracing tools like OpenTelemetry or Zipkin to gain insights into the performance of microservices architectures.

6. **Log Retention and Rotation:** Define log retention and rotation policies to manage log data efficiently, comply with regulations, and optimize storage costs.

7. **Data Security:** Secure access to monitoring and alerting data by implementing authentication, authorization, and encryption mechanisms.

8. **Documentation:** Document the architecture and configuration of monitoring and alerting solutions to facilitate troubleshooting and onboarding of new team members.

9. **Automated Remediation:** Integrate monitoring tools with automation frameworks to trigger automated responses to common issues.

Monitoring and alerting automation are essential practices in

DevOps, providing the visibility and insights needed to maintain the reliability and performance of modern applications and infrastructure. By selecting the right tools, defining clear monitoring and alerting strategies, and adhering to best practices, organizations can proactively manage their systems, troubleshoot issues efficiently, and continuously optimize their operations.

CHAPTER 5

Fostering a DevOps Culture of Collaboration

DevOps is not merely about tools and processes; it's a transformative culture that reshapes how teams collaborate to deliver software. DevOps culture and collaboration are the cornerstones of this paradigm shift, emphasizing shared goals, open communication, and a commitment to continuous improvement. In this introductory exploration of DevOps culture and collaboration, we'll delve into the foundational principles, the cultural shifts it necessitates, and the vital role it plays in achieving the seamless integration of development and operations teams. It's a culture that places people at its core, nurturing a collaborative spirit that fuels innovation and drives organizations towards their digital transformation goals.

A. Building a DevOps Team: Orchestrating Collaboration and Expertise

A successful DevOps transformation hinges on assembling a dedicated and well-structured DevOps team that embodies the core principles of collaboration, automation, and continuous improvement. This team serves as the driving force behind the adoption of DevOps practices and the integration of development and operations. In this comprehensive exploration of building a DevOps team, we'll delve into the crucial components, roles, and strategies necessary to create a high-performing DevOps team.

Key Components of a DevOps Team:

1. **Collaboration:** A DevOps team is characterized by its ability to collaborate seamlessly across traditionally siloed development and operations functions. Open communication and teamwork are essential.

2. **Automation Expertise:** Team members should possess expertise in automation tools and technologies, enabling them to automate processes and tasks effectively.

3. **Diverse Skill Set:** A well-rounded DevOps team should include individuals with expertise in development, operations, security, and other relevant areas.

4. **Continuous Learning:** DevOps is an ever-evolving field. Team members should have a growth mindset, a willingness to learn, and a commitment to staying updated on industry trends.

Roles in a DevOps Team:

1. **DevOps Engineer:** DevOps engineers are the architects of automation, responsible for designing and implementing automation pipelines, infrastructure as code (IaC), and

integration between development and operations tools.

2. **Release Manager:** Release managers oversee the deployment and release processes, ensuring that releases are well-coordinated, tested, and meet quality standards.

3. **Continuous Integration/Continuous Deployment (CI/CD) Specialist:** These specialists focus on setting up and maintaining CI/CD pipelines, automating the build and deployment processes, and ensuring code is delivered reliably and rapidly.

4. **Site Reliability Engineer (SRE):** SREs are responsible for ensuring the reliability and performance of applications in production. They use automation to monitor, respond to incidents, and manage system reliability.

5. **Security Champion:** Security champions embed security best practices within the DevOps pipeline, identifying and mitigating security vulnerabilities and ensuring compliance with security standards.

6. **Quality Assurance (QA) Engineer:** QA engineers work alongside development teams to automate testing, enabling rapid and reliable feedback on code changes.

Strategies for Building a High-Performing DevOps Team:

1. **Skills Assessment:** Identify the existing skills within your

organization and determine the gaps that need to be filled. Offer training and development opportunities to bridge these gaps.

2. **Cross-Functional Collaboration:** Foster a culture of collaboration by breaking down silos and encouraging open communication between development, operations, and other teams.

3. **Hiring and Recruitment:** When hiring, look for individuals who not only possess technical skills but also exhibit a collaborative mindset and adaptability.

4. **Mentoring and Knowledge Sharing:** Establish mentoring programs within the team to facilitate knowledge sharing and skill development among team members.

5. **Diversity and Inclusion:** Embrace diversity in your team, as it brings different perspectives and experiences that can enhance problem-solving and creativity.

6. **Tools and Automation:** Invest in automation tools that simplify repetitive tasks, streamline workflows, and promote collaboration.

7. **Culture of Continuous Improvement:** Encourage a culture of continuous learning and improvement, where team members are empowered to suggest and implement process

enhancements.

8. **Measurement and Metrics:** Define key performance indicators (KPIs) to measure the success of your DevOps initiatives and track progress over time.

9. **Documentation:** Document processes, procedures, and configurations to ensure consistency and facilitate knowledge transfer.

10. **Leadership Support:** Ensure that leadership is committed to and supportive of the DevOps transformation, providing the necessary resources and removing obstacles.

Building a DevOps team is not just about assembling individuals with technical skills; it's about creating a culture of collaboration, automation, and continuous learning. By carefully selecting team members, defining roles, and fostering a collaborative environment, organizations can cultivate a high-performing DevOps team capable of driving innovation, accelerating delivery, and ensuring the reliability of their software and infrastructure.

B. Communication and Collaboration Practices in DevOps: Weaving the Fabric of Efficiency and Innovation

Effective communication and collaboration are the lifeblood of

DevOps, enabling cross-functional teams to work together seamlessly to deliver high-quality software rapidly. DevOps thrives on the principle of breaking down silos between development, operations, and other stakeholders, fostering a culture of shared responsibility and continuous improvement. In this in-depth exploration of communication and collaboration practices in DevOps, we'll delve into the key principles, strategies, and tools that facilitate cohesive teamwork and drive innovation.

Key Principles of Communication and Collaboration in DevOps:

1. **Shared Objectives:** Teams should align around common objectives and shared goals, focusing on delivering value to the customer rather than individual or departmental priorities.

2. **Transparency:** Open and transparent communication ensures that all team members have access to the same information, promoting trust and collaboration.

3. **Frequent Feedback:** Regular feedback loops enable teams to iterate quickly, identify issues, and make necessary adjustments throughout the software development and delivery process.

4. **Cross-Functional Teams:** DevOps promotes the formation of cross-functional teams that include members with diverse skills and expertise, allowing for end-to-end ownership of

projects.

Strategies for Effective Communication and Collaboration:

1. **Daily Standup Meetings:** Hold daily standup meetings (e.g., Scrum or Kanban daily standups) where team members share progress, discuss obstacles, and plan their work for the day.

2. **Collaborative Tools:** Utilize collaboration and communication tools like Slack, Microsoft Teams, or Atlassian's Confluence and Jira to facilitate real-time conversations, document sharing, and project tracking.

3. **ChatOps:** Integrate chat platforms with automation scripts and tools to execute tasks, monitor systems, and respond to alerts directly from chat interfaces.

4. **Cross-Training:** Encourage team members to cross-train and gain knowledge in areas outside their core expertise, enabling them to better understand and support other team members.

5. **Documentation:** Maintain comprehensive documentation, including runbooks and playbooks, to ensure that processes are well-documented and accessible to all team members.

6. **Post-Incident Reviews:** Conduct post-incident reviews (blameless retrospectives) to analyze and learn from incidents, share insights, and improve incident response.

7. **Pair Programming:** Foster pair programming and code reviews to encourage collaboration, share knowledge, and improve code quality.

8. **Infrastructure as Code (IaC):** Implement IaC practices to define infrastructure and configuration in code, making it easier for teams to collaborate on infrastructure changes.

9. **DevOps Days and Hackathons:** Organize events like DevOps Days and hackathons to bring together cross-functional teams to work on innovative projects and foster collaboration.

Tools for Communication and Collaboration:

1. **Slack:** A popular team messaging and collaboration platform that enables real-time communication and integrates with various tools and services.

2. **Microsoft Teams:** A communication and collaboration platform within the Microsoft 365 suite that offers chat, video conferencing, and document sharing.

3. **Jira and Confluence:** Atlassian's tools for project tracking, issue management, and collaborative documentation.

4. **Git and Version Control Systems:** Version control systems like Git enable teams to collaborate on code and track changes efficiently.

5. **Video Conferencing Tools:** Platforms like Zoom, Microsoft Teams, and Google Meet facilitate virtual meetings and screen sharing for remote collaboration.

6. **Project Management Tools:** Tools like Trello, Asana, or Monday.com help teams organize and manage tasks and projects.

7. **Collaborative Code Editors:** Tools like Visual Studio Code with Live Share enable real-time collaborative coding sessions.

8. **Wiki Platforms:** Wiki platforms like MediaWiki or DokuWiki are valuable for creating and sharing documentation within teams.

Effective communication and collaboration practices lie at the heart of DevOps, enabling teams to break down traditional barriers and accelerate software delivery. By fostering a culture of openness, transparency, and continuous feedback, DevOps organizations can harness the power of collaboration to drive innovation, increase efficiency, and deliver value to their customers consistently.

C. Encouraging a Culture of Experimentation and Learning in DevOps: Fueling Continuous Improvement

In the dynamic landscape of DevOps, embracing a culture of experimentation and learning is not just an option; it's a necessity. This culture fosters innovation, drives continuous improvement, and empowers teams to adapt and thrive in an ever-evolving tech ecosystem. In this in-depth exploration, we'll delve into the principles, benefits, and strategies for cultivating a culture of experimentation and learning in the world of DevOps.

Principles of a Culture of Experimentation and Learning:

1. **Openness to Change:** Embrace change as an opportunity for growth and progress, rather than fearing it as a disruptor.

2. **Continuous Improvement:** Encourage teams to regularly reflect on their processes and outcomes, seeking ways to enhance efficiency and effectiveness.

3. **Risk-Tolerance:** Create an environment where taking calculated risks is encouraged, and failure is seen as a stepping stone toward success.

4. **Data-Driven Decision-Making:** Use data and metrics to guide decisions, measure the impact of changes, and validate assumptions.

5. **Collaboration:** Promote cross-functional collaboration and

knowledge sharing, enabling teams to learn from one another's experiences.

Benefits of a Culture of Experimentation and Learning:

1. **Innovation:** Experimentation fosters innovation by encouraging teams to explore new ideas and approaches.

2. **Adaptability:** Teams that are open to learning can adapt quickly to changing circumstances and technologies.

3. **Continuous Evolution:** A culture of experimentation and learning ensures that processes and practices are constantly evolving and improving.

4. **Employee Engagement:** Encouraging learning and experimentation can boost employee engagement and job satisfaction.

Strategies for Cultivating a Culture of Experimentation and Learning:

1. **Lead by Example:** Leaders should demonstrate a commitment to learning and experimentation, setting the tone for the organization.

2. **Create Safe Spaces:** Encourage experimentation by creating safe environments where employees feel comfortable taking risks and making mistakes.

3. **Dedicated Time:** Allow employees dedicated time for learning and innovation, such as hackathons or innovation sprints.

4. **Cross-Functional Teams:** Form cross-functional teams that bring together diverse perspectives and skill sets to tackle complex challenges.

5. **Mentorship and Coaching:** Provide mentorship and coaching to help employees grow in their roles and develop new skills.

6. **Celebrate Learning:** Recognize and celebrate the successes and learning experiences that come from experimentation, even if they result in failure.

7. **Feedback Loops:** Implement feedback loops that enable teams to continuously learn from their experiences and adjust their approaches.

8. **Learning Resources:** Provide access to learning resources such as online courses, workshops, and conferences.

9. **Knowledge Sharing:** Encourage knowledge sharing through internal documentation, presentations, and knowledge-sharing sessions.

10. **Experimentation Frameworks:** Develop frameworks for structured experimentation, including hypothesis formulation,

testing, and analysis.

Tools and Technologies for Experimentation and Learning:

1. **A/B Testing Platforms:** Tools like Optimizely and Google Optimize enable controlled experiments to optimize user experiences.

2. **Collaboration and Communication Tools:** Platforms like Slack and Microsoft Teams facilitate real-time communication and knowledge sharing.

3. **Learning Management Systems (LMS):** LMS platforms like Moodle and Canvas support employee training and development.

4. **Analytics and Data Visualization Tools:** Tools like Google Analytics and Tableau help teams analyze and visualize data to derive insights.

5. **Experimentation Platforms:** Platforms like Split.io and LaunchDarkly provide feature flagging and experimentation capabilities.

6. **Online Learning Platforms:** Platforms like Coursera, edX, and Pluralsight offer a wide range of online courses for skill development.

A culture of experimentation and learning is a foundational

pillar of DevOps, enabling organizations to adapt, innovate, and deliver value to customers continuously. By fostering an environment where curiosity, risk-taking, and knowledge sharing are encouraged, DevOps teams can unlock their full potential, stay at the forefront of technological advancements, and drive their organizations toward excellence in the digital age.

D. Measuring and Improving Collaboration in DevOps: The Path to Efficiency and Innovation

In DevOps, collaboration is not just a buzzword; it's a fundamental principle that underpins the entire methodology. Effective collaboration among development, operations, and other teams is essential for delivering high-quality software at speed. However, it's not enough to simply encourage collaboration; organizations must also measure it and continually seek ways to improve it. In this comprehensive exploration, we'll delve into the importance of measuring and improving collaboration in DevOps, the key metrics to track, and strategies for fostering a culture of effective collaboration.

The Importance of Measuring Collaboration in DevOps:

1. **Visibility:** Measuring collaboration provides visibility into how effectively teams are working together and where bottlenecks or challenges may exist.

2. **Continuous Improvement:** Metrics provide a baseline for improvement efforts, enabling teams to track progress and make data-driven adjustments.

3. **Efficiency:** Effective collaboration reduces delays, rework, and miscommunications, leading to faster delivery and lower operational costs.

4. **Quality:** Collaboration impacts the quality of deliverables, as cross-functional teams can catch issues earlier in the development process.

Key Metrics for Measuring Collaboration:

1. **Lead Time:** The time it takes from the initiation of a work item (e.g., a user story or bug report) to its completion. Longer lead times may indicate inefficiencies in collaboration.

2. **Cycle Time:** The time it takes to complete a single unit of work, often measured from when development starts to when it's deployed to production.

3. **Deployment Frequency:** The rate at which changes are deployed to production. Higher deployment frequency is often a sign of streamlined collaboration.

4. **Change Failure Rate:** The percentage of changes that result in issues or incidents in production. Effective collaboration should lead to a lower failure rate.

5. **Incident Resolution Time:** The time it takes to resolve incidents or outages in production. Collaboration can impact how quickly issues are identified and addressed.

6. **Code Review Efficiency:** Metrics related to code reviews, such as the time taken to complete a code review or the number of iterations required, can indicate collaboration effectiveness.

7. **Team Satisfaction:** Regular surveys or feedback mechanisms can gauge team members' satisfaction with collaboration processes and tools.

Strategies for Improving Collaboration in DevOps:

1. **Cross-Functional Teams:** Encourage the formation of cross-functional teams that include members from different departments and skill sets, fostering collaboration from the outset.

2. **Collaboration Tools:** Invest in collaboration tools that facilitate real-time communication, document sharing, and workflow integration, such as Slack, Microsoft Teams, or Confluence.

3. **Shared Objectives:** Ensure that teams have shared objectives and a clear understanding of their roles in achieving those objectives.

4. **Feedback Culture:** Foster a culture of open and constructive

feedback, where team members feel comfortable sharing their thoughts and concerns.

5. **Collaboration Training:** Provide training on effective collaboration techniques and tools to ensure teams are making the most of available resources.

6. **DevOps Practices:** Implement DevOps practices like continuous integration, continuous delivery, and automation to streamline collaboration processes.

7. **Regular Retrospectives:** Conduct regular retrospectives or post-mortems to assess and improve collaboration after significant projects or incidents.

8. **Knowledge Sharing:** Encourage knowledge sharing through documentation, presentations, and knowledge-sharing sessions.

9. **Mentorship and Coaching:** Offer mentorship and coaching programs to help team members develop collaboration skills and grow in their roles.

10. **Leadership Support:** Ensure that leadership is committed to and supportive of collaboration initiatives, providing the necessary resources and removing obstacles.

Measuring and Improving Collaboration Tools:

1. **Collaboration Platforms:** Tools like Slack, Microsoft Teams, and Atlassian's suite (Confluence, Jira) provide features for tracking communication and document sharing.

2. **Project Management Tools:** Platforms like Trello, Asana, and Monday.com can help teams manage tasks and projects collaboratively.

3. **Version Control Systems:** Git and other version control systems offer insights into how teams collaborate on code.

4. **Feedback Tools:** Use feedback collection tools like surveys or anonymous feedback channels to gather input on collaboration effectiveness.

Measuring and improving collaboration is not just a one-time effort but an ongoing process in DevOps. By tracking key metrics, implementing effective strategies, and fostering a culture of open communication and teamwork, organizations can enhance their collaboration capabilities, reduce friction in their processes, and ultimately deliver value to customers more efficiently and effectively.

CHAPTER 6

Infrastructure as Code (IaC)

In the fast-paced world of DevOps, where agility and automation are paramount, Infrastructure as Code (IaC) stands as a transformative concept. IaC revolutionizes the way organizations provision, configure, and manage their infrastructure by treating it as code, bringing the benefits of versioning, automation, and repeatability to the realm of infrastructure management. In this introductory exploration of IaC, we'll delve into its fundamental principles, its significance in the DevOps ecosystem, and the immense potential it holds for optimizing infrastructure deployment and management.

A. Introduction to Infrastructure as Code (IaC): Building a Foundation for Agile Operations

In the dynamic landscape of modern IT operations, Infrastructure as Code (IaC) has emerged as a transformative practice that redefines how infrastructure is provisioned, configured, and managed. IaC treats infrastructure elements such as servers, networks, and databases as code, enabling automation, version control, and rapid scalability. In this comprehensive exploration of IaC, we will delve into its definition, principles, benefits, and practical applications within the context of DevOps and agile operations.

Definition of Infrastructure as Code (IaC):

Infrastructure as Code (IaC) is an approach to infrastructure management in which infrastructure components and their configurations are defined and managed through code, typically in a declarative or scripting language. This code-based representation allows for automated provisioning, configuration, and maintenance of infrastructure resources.

Key Principles of Infrastructure as Code:

1. **Automation:** IaC automates the process of provisioning and configuring infrastructure, reducing manual intervention and minimizing the risk of human errors.

2. **Version Control:** IaC code is stored in version control systems, enabling teams to track changes, collaborate effectively, and roll back to previous configurations if needed.

3. **Consistency:** IaC ensures that infrastructure is consistent across environments, eliminating configuration drift and ensuring predictable behavior.

4. **Scalability:** With IaC, it is easy to scale infrastructure up or down based on demand, making it highly adaptable to

changing workloads.

5. **Reproducibility:** IaC enables the recreation of infrastructure environments quickly and accurately, which is crucial for testing, development, and disaster recovery scenarios.

Benefits of Infrastructure as Code:

1. **Agility:** IaC allows organizations to respond quickly to changing business requirements by rapidly provisioning and adapting infrastructure resources.

2. **Reduced Manual Work:** Automation through IaC reduces the need for manual provisioning and configuration, freeing up IT personnel for more strategic tasks.

3. **Consistency and Reliability:** IaC ensures that infrastructure configurations are consistent, leading to greater reliability and fewer configuration-related issues.

4. **Versioning and Rollback:** IaC code is versioned, enabling teams to track changes and easily roll back to previous configurations in case of problems.

5. **Cost Optimization:** IaC can help optimize costs by automating resource scaling and eliminating unused or underutilized resources.

Practical Applications of Infrastructure as Code:

1. **Cloud Resource Management:** IaC is widely used to provision and manage cloud resources on platforms such as AWS, Azure, and Google Cloud.

2. **Container Orchestration:** IaC is essential for defining and managing containerized applications and their underlying infrastructure using platforms like Kubernetes.

3. **Configuration Management:** IaC tools like Ansible, Puppet, and Chef automate the configuration of servers and applications.

4. **DevOps Pipelines:** IaC is integrated into CI/CD pipelines to automate the deployment of infrastructure alongside application code.

5. **Testing Environments:** IaC is valuable for creating and managing consistent testing environments, ensuring that tests are conducted on reliable infrastructure.

Popular Infrastructure as Code Tools:

1. **Terraform:** An open-source IaC tool by HashiCorp that enables the provisioning and management of infrastructure resources across various cloud providers and services.

2. **AWS CloudFormation:** Amazon Web Services' native IaC

service for defining and provisioning AWS infrastructure.

3. **Azure Resource Manager (ARM) Templates:** Microsoft Azure's IaC solution for deploying and managing Azure resources.

4. **Ansible:** A configuration management and automation tool that includes IaC capabilities for managing infrastructure and applications.

5. **Chef and Puppet:** Configuration management tools that offer IaC capabilities for automating server and application configurations.

Infrastructure as Code represents a fundamental shift in how organizations manage their infrastructure, aligning perfectly with the principles of DevOps and agile operations. By adopting IaC practices and leveraging the right tools, businesses can gain agility, reliability, and cost efficiency, enabling them to meet the ever-evolving demands of the digital age with ease and confidence.

B. IaC Tools: Harnessing the Power of Terraform, Ansible, and More

Infrastructure as Code (IaC) is a pivotal component of modern DevOps practices, enabling organizations to automate infrastructure provisioning, configuration, and management.

While numerous IaC tools are available, two of the most popular and widely adopted are Terraform and Ansible. In this comprehensive exploration, we'll delve into these IaC tools, understanding their strengths, use cases, and how they contribute to the efficiency and agility of DevOps workflows.

Terraform: Infrastructure Provisioning and Orchestration

Terraform, developed by HashiCorp, is a declarative IaC tool designed for infrastructure provisioning and orchestration. It provides a unified language for describing infrastructure components across various cloud providers and on-premises environments. Key features and concepts of Terraform include:

1. Declarative Language: Terraform uses a declarative configuration language, HashiCorp Configuration Language (HCL), allowing users to describe their desired infrastructure state without specifying the step-by-step procedures to achieve it.

2. Provider Ecosystem: Terraform supports a wide range of cloud providers and services, including AWS, Azure, Google Cloud, and more. Providers offer pre-built resources and configurations for these platforms.

3. Resource Graph: Terraform builds a resource graph that represents dependencies between infrastructure components. It determines the optimal order for provisioning and managing resources.

4. Plan and Apply: Terraform's workflow involves two main commands: "terraform plan" generates an execution plan, while "terraform apply" enacts the plan to create or modify infrastructure.

5. State Management: Terraform maintains a state file that records the current state of the infrastructure. This file is used to track changes and ensure consistency.

Use Cases for Terraform:

- **Multi-Cloud Deployments:** Terraform excels at managing infrastructure across multiple cloud providers, making it a top choice for organizations with multi-cloud strategies.

- **Infrastructure Automation:** It is used to automate the provisioning of servers, databases, networking components, and other infrastructure elements.

- **Container Orchestration:** Terraform can provision and manage resources for container orchestration platforms like Kubernetes.

- **Immutable Infrastructure:** Organizations implementing immutable infrastructure can use Terraform to define and deploy new infrastructure versions consistently.

Ansible: Configuration Management and Automation

Ansible, developed by Red Hat, is a powerful open-source automation tool that serves as both a configuration management tool and an IaC solution. It uses a declarative language to define infrastructure and application configurations, making it agentless and easy to set up. Key features and concepts of Ansible include:

1. **Playbooks:** Ansible configurations are defined in playbooks, which are YAML files that specify desired states and tasks to be executed on target systems.

2. **Agentless:** Ansible operates over SSH or PowerShell, without requiring agents to be installed on target machines, which simplifies setup and management.

3. **Idempotent Tasks:** Ansible playbooks are idempotent, meaning they can be run multiple times without causing unintended changes to the system.

4. **Extensible Modules:** Ansible provides a vast library of pre-built modules for common tasks, and users can create custom modules to extend functionality.

5. **Dynamic Inventories:** Ansible can automatically discover and manage hosts through dynamic inventories, making it suitable for dynamic and cloud-based environments.

Use Cases for Ansible:

- **Configuration Management:** Ansible is widely used for configuring and maintaining servers, ensuring consistent and reliable system configurations.

- **Application Deployment:** It can automate the deployment of applications, including the installation and configuration of required dependencies.

- **Orchestration:** Ansible orchestrates complex workflows and tasks, coordinating actions across multiple systems.

- **Security Automation:** Ansible can be employed for security tasks such as patch management, vulnerability scanning, and compliance checks.

- **Continuous Integration/Continuous Deployment (CI/CD):** Ansible can be integrated into CI/CD pipelines to automate deployment and configuration tasks.

Choosing Between Terraform and Ansible:

- **Terraform** is primarily focused on infrastructure provisioning and is an excellent choice for defining and managing cloud resources.

- **Ansible** offers a broader range of capabilities, including configuration management and application deployment, making it suitable for both infrastructure and application automation.

- **Integration:** Many organizations use both Terraform and Ansible in conjunction. Terraform provisions infrastructure, while Ansible configures and manages the software running on that infrastructure.

In summary, Terraform and Ansible are two powerful IaC tools that cater to different aspects of infrastructure and automation within the DevOps ecosystem. Organizations often leverage both tools to create a comprehensive and flexible automation solution that optimizes infrastructure deployment, configuration, and management while promoting efficiency and collaboration across teams.

C. Infrastructure Provisioning: The Foundation of Agile Operations

Infrastructure provisioning is a critical aspect of modern IT operations, enabling organizations to create and manage the computing resources necessary for their applications and services. In the context of DevOps and Infrastructure as Code (IaC), provisioning is a fundamental process that underpins the dynamic and scalable nature of cloud-native environments. In this comprehensive exploration, we'll delve into the significance of infrastructure provisioning, its key principles, methods, and the role it plays in enabling agile operations.

Significance of Infrastructure Provisioning:

Infrastructure provisioning is a cornerstone of modern IT operations, and its importance cannot be overstated for several reasons:

1. **Agility:** Provisioning enables organizations to rapidly respond to changing business needs by quickly deploying or scaling computing resources. This agility is crucial in today's fast-paced digital landscape.

2. **Efficiency:** Automated provisioning processes reduce manual intervention, minimize errors, and optimize resource utilization, leading to cost savings and operational efficiency.

3. **Scalability:** Provisioning allows organizations to scale their infrastructure up or down to accommodate variable workloads and traffic spikes, ensuring optimal performance and resource allocation.

4. **Consistency:** With Infrastructure as Code (IaC) principles, provisioning ensures that infrastructure configurations are consistent across environments, reducing the risk of configuration drift and improving reliability.

Key Principles of Infrastructure Provisioning:

1. **Automation:** Automation is at the heart of provisioning. Infrastructure can be provisioned automatically using scripts, templates, or IaC tools to eliminate manual steps and reduce human error.

2. **Idempotency:** Provisioning processes should be idempotent, meaning that running them multiple times does not produce unintended changes. This ensures that infrastructure remains in the desired state.

3. **State Management:** Maintaining a record of the infrastructure's current state is essential. Tools like Terraform or AWS CloudFormation use state files to track the state of provisioned resources.

4. **Scalability:** Provisioning should support scalability by allowing organizations to add or remove resources based on demand, enabling elasticity in cloud environments.

Methods of Infrastructure Provisioning:

1. **Manual Provisioning:** In traditional IT environments, infrastructure provisioning was often a manual process involving physical servers and manual configurations. While this approach is still used, it is less common in modern cloud-native environments.

2. **Scripting:** Many organizations use scripting languages like Bash, PowerShell, or Python to automate provisioning tasks. Scripts can be customized to meet specific infrastructure requirements.

3. **Configuration Management Tools:** Tools like Ansible, Puppet, and Chef are not only used for configuration management but also for provisioning. They can automate the setup and configuration of servers and applications.

4. **IaC Tools:** Infrastructure as Code (IaC) tools such as Terraform, AWS CloudFormation, and Azure Resource Manager Templates are designed specifically for infrastructure provisioning. They use declarative code to define the desired infrastructure state and automatically provision resources accordingly.

5. **Container Orchestration:** Container orchestration platforms like Kubernetes can provision containers and manage the underlying infrastructure required to run them.

Role of Infrastructure Provisioning in DevOps:

Infrastructure provisioning plays a pivotal role in the DevOps methodology by enabling the rapid and automated deployment of infrastructure resources as part of continuous integration and continuous deployment (CI/CD) pipelines. This integration of provisioning into the DevOps workflow ensures that infrastructure changes are as agile and automated as software code changes, allowing for faster and more reliable releases.

In conclusion, infrastructure provisioning is a foundational process that empowers organizations to create, manage, and scale their computing resources efficiently and effectively. In the context of DevOps and IaC, provisioning becomes a dynamic and automated part of the agile operations ecosystem, driving innovation and ensuring that infrastructure aligns seamlessly with changing business needs.

D. IaC Best Practices: Building Reliable and Scalable Infrastructure as Code

Infrastructure as Code (IaC) is a powerful approach to managing and provisioning infrastructure in a programmable and automated manner. When implemented with best practices in mind, IaC can lead to more efficient, reliable, and scalable infrastructure deployments. In this in-depth exploration, we will delve into the key best practices for IaC, empowering you to harness its full potential while minimizing potential pitfalls.

1. Use Version Control:

Just like application code, IaC code should be stored in version control systems (e.g., Git). This practice enables collaboration, change tracking, and rollbacks to previous states. It also ensures that your infrastructure code is treated with the same level of care as software code.

2. Modularize Your Code:

Break down your IaC code into modular components and reusable modules. This approach promotes maintainability and reusability while making it easier to manage complex infrastructure configurations.

3. Follow a Declarative Approach:

Adopt a declarative approach in your IaC code, where you specify the desired end state of your infrastructure rather than the sequence of actions to reach that state. Declarative IaC code is more idempotent and less error-prone.

4. Leverage IaC Tools:

Choose the right IaC tool for your needs. Popular options like Terraform, AWS CloudFormation, and Ansible offer various capabilities and integrations. Select a tool that aligns with your infrastructure requirements and the platforms you use.

5. Use Variables and Parameterization:

Parameterize your IaC code by using variables and parameters. This makes your code more flexible, allowing you to customize infrastructure configurations for different environments or use cases without modifying the code itself.

6. Maintain Separation of Concerns:

Separate infrastructure concerns into distinct code modules or layers. This includes separating network configurations, security settings, application deployments, and other aspects. This separation enhances maintainability and reduces the risk of unintentional changes.

7. Implement Testing and Validation:

Test your IaC code thoroughly. Implement automated tests and validation checks to ensure that your infrastructure is provisioned correctly and consistently. This includes unit tests, integration tests, and validation against compliance and security standards.

8. Adopt Infrastructure as Data:

Consider treating your infrastructure as data. This involves using data structures, templates, or configuration files to define your infrastructure resources. This approach can make it easier to manage complex infrastructure setups.

9. Document Your Code:

Comprehensive documentation is essential for IaC projects. Document the purpose, usage, and any special considerations for your IaC code. Include information about variables, modules, and resource dependencies.

10. Implement Code Reviews:

Incorporate code reviews into your IaC development process. Code reviews ensure that your infrastructure code aligns with best practices, security standards, and organizational guidelines.

11. Secure Secrets and Sensitive Data:

Handle secrets and sensitive data carefully. Use secure vaults or key management systems to store and manage secrets, and avoid hardcoding sensitive information in your IaC code.

12. Plan for Disaster Recovery:

Include disaster recovery considerations in your IaC code. Ensure that you can recreate your infrastructure quickly in the event of a failure or disaster, and regularly test your recovery procedures.

13. Monitor and Audit Changes:

Implement monitoring and auditing of your IaC deployments. Track changes to your infrastructure configurations and use monitoring tools to detect issues and anomalies.

14. Keep Abreast of Updates:

Stay updated with the latest versions of your IaC tools and the underlying infrastructure platforms. Regularly update your IaC code to incorporate new features, security patches, and improvements.

15. Automate Workflows:

Integrate IaC into your CI/CD pipelines to automate infrastructure changes. This ensures that infrastructure changes are tested, deployed, and validated consistently and rapidly.

By adhering to these IaC best practices, organizations can realize the full potential of IaC, including increased reliability, scalability, and agility in managing infrastructure. These practices help mitigate risks, reduce errors, and streamline the process of provisioning and maintaining infrastructure, ultimately contributing to the success of DevOps initiatives.

E. Immutable Infrastructure: Enhancing Reliability and Security in DevOps

Immutable infrastructure is a concept that has gained significant traction in the world of DevOps and cloud-native environments. It challenges the traditional approach to infrastructure management by promoting the idea that infrastructure components should never be modified once they are deployed. Instead, any changes or updates result in the creation of entirely new, pristine instances. In this comprehensive exploration, we'll delve into the principles, benefits, and practical considerations of immutable infrastructure and its role in improving reliability, security, and efficiency.

Principles of Immutable Infrastructure:

1. **Immutable, Not Mutable:** In the context of immutable infrastructure, "immutable" means unchangeable. Once an infrastructure component, such as a virtual machine or container, is deployed, it is never modified. Any updates or changes are implemented by creating new, updated instances.

2. **Versioned Artifacts:** Infrastructure components are treated as versioned artifacts. Instead of modifying existing instances, new instances are created from predefined, versioned templates or images.

3. **Disposable Resources:** Infrastructure instances are considered disposable. When changes or updates are needed, the existing instances are terminated, and new ones are launched to replace them. This practice ensures that instances remain in a consistent, known state.

Benefits of Immutable Infrastructure:

1. **Enhanced Reliability:** Immutable infrastructure reduces the risk of configuration drift and unintended changes. Each instance is known to be in a pristine state, reducing the

likelihood of issues caused by differences between instances.

2. **Scalability:** Immutable infrastructure simplifies scaling because new instances can be launched quickly and consistently. Auto-scaling groups can be used to automatically manage instance counts based on demand.

3. **Simplified Rollbacks:** In case of issues or errors, rollbacks are straightforward. You can revert to a previous version of the infrastructure by launching instances from the previous version's template.

4. **Security:** Immutable infrastructure enhances security by ensuring that instances are regularly replaced with updated and patched versions, reducing exposure to vulnerabilities.

5. **Predictable Testing:** Testing is more predictable because you're working with known, consistent states. This is valuable for quality assurance and can lead to fewer production issues.

6. **Audit Trail:** Changes to infrastructure are recorded through version control systems, providing an audit trail of all changes and updates.

Practical Considerations for Implementing Immutable Infrastructure:

1. **Automation:** Immutable infrastructure relies heavily on automation. Infrastructure components should be defined as

code using IaC tools like Terraform or AWS CloudFormation, and deployment pipelines should automate the process of creating new instances.

2. **Continuous Integration/Continuous Deployment (CI/CD):** Immutable infrastructure integrates seamlessly with CI/CD pipelines. New versions of infrastructure templates are automatically built, tested, and deployed when code changes occur.

3. **Version Control:** Infrastructure templates, such as Amazon Machine Images (AMIs) or Docker images, should be versioned and stored in version control systems. This ensures that you can recreate any past version when needed.

4. **Monitoring and Logging:** Robust monitoring and logging are crucial for identifying issues, assessing performance, and tracking changes to the infrastructure.

5. **Testing:** Rigorous testing is essential to validate new versions of infrastructure templates. Automated testing should include functional, security, and performance testing.

6. **Security Patching:** Ensure that new instances are launched with the latest security patches and updates. Regularly update your infrastructure templates to include these patches.

7. **Rollback Procedures:** Establish clear and well-documented

rollback procedures in case of issues with new versions of infrastructure.

8. **Backups and Data Preservation:** Implement strategies for data backup and preservation when transitioning to new instances to avoid data loss.

Immutable infrastructure represents a paradigm shift in how infrastructure is managed and updated. It aligns closely with the principles of automation, version control, and reliability that are central to DevOps practices. By embracing immutable infrastructure, organizations can significantly enhance the resilience, security, and efficiency of their IT environments, ultimately leading to more reliable and secure services for their users.

CHAPTER 7

DevOps Security

In the ever-evolving landscape of software development and IT operations, security is a paramount concern. DevOps, with its emphasis on speed, automation, and collaboration, has revolutionized how organizations deliver software. However, with increased velocity comes the need for enhanced security measures to safeguard against vulnerabilities and threats. This introductory exploration of DevOps Security, often referred to as DevSecOps, will delve into the critical role of security in DevOps practices, the key principles that underpin it, and the strategies for integrating security seamlessly into the DevOps pipeline.

A. Security in the DevOps Pipeline: Protecting the Continuous Delivery Process

Security in the DevOps pipeline, often referred to as "DevSecOps," is a critical practice that integrates security measures and best practices seamlessly into the entire software development and delivery process. DevOps accelerates the development and deployment of software, but this velocity should not come at the expense of security. In this in-depth exploration, we'll delve into the key principles, practices, and strategies for ensuring security at every stage of the DevOps pipeline.

Principles of Security in the DevOps Pipeline:

1. **Shift Left:** One fundamental principle of DevSecOps is to "shift left," which means addressing security concerns as early as possible in the software development lifecycle. By identifying and addressing security issues during the design and coding phases, teams can prevent vulnerabilities from propagating through the pipeline.

2. **Automation:** Automation is a cornerstone of DevOps, and it applies equally to security. Automated security testing, vulnerability scanning, and compliance checks can be integrated into CI/CD pipelines to ensure that security assessments are performed consistently and rapidly.

3. **Continuous Monitoring:** Security is not a one-time activity; it's an ongoing process. Continuous monitoring of applications and infrastructure for security threats and vulnerabilities is essential. This includes real-time alerting and auditing of system behavior.

Security Practices in the DevOps Pipeline:

1. **Code Scanning:** Incorporate static code analysis tools into the development phase to identify security issues in the source code. These tools can catch common vulnerabilities such as

SQL injection or cross-site scripting (XSS).

2. **Dependency Scanning:** Utilize dependency scanning tools to identify and remediate vulnerabilities in third-party libraries and components used in your application. Outdated or vulnerable dependencies can be a significant security risk.

3. **Container Security:** If you're using containers, ensure container images are scanned for vulnerabilities before deployment. Tools like Clair or Trivy can check container images for known security issues.

4. **Automated Testing:** Implement automated security testing, including dynamic application security testing (DAST) and runtime application self-protection (RASP). These tools assess applications while they are running to identify and mitigate security threats.

5. **Infrastructure as Code (IaC) Security:** Integrate security checks into your IaC templates and scripts to ensure that infrastructure configurations are compliant with security policies. Tools like Terrascan and Checkov can help with IaC security checks.

6. **Continuous Compliance:** Automate compliance checks to ensure that applications and infrastructure meet regulatory and security standards. Compliance as code (CaaC) is a practice that codifies compliance requirements into IaC templates.

7. **Secrets Management:** Securely manage secrets, credentials, and API keys. Use dedicated secrets management solutions like HashiCorp Vault or AWS Secrets Manager to protect sensitive information.

8. **Access Control:** Enforce strong access controls and least privilege principles. Implement role-based access control (RBAC) and regularly review and update permissions.

Integrating Security into the DevOps Pipeline:

1. **Security Gates:** Introduce security gates in your CI/CD pipeline. These gates halt the pipeline if certain security criteria are not met. For example, a vulnerability scan could be a mandatory gate before deployment.

2. **Education and Training:** Ensure that development and operations teams receive training on security best practices and threats. Security awareness is crucial for making informed decisions and taking proactive security measures.

3. **Collaboration:** Foster collaboration between development, operations, and security teams. Cross-functional collaboration ensures that security considerations are addressed holistically.

4. **Incident Response Plan:** Develop an incident response plan that outlines how security incidents are detected, reported, and responded to. Test and refine this plan regularly.

5. **Continuous Improvement:** Security is an ongoing process. Regularly assess and refine your security practices based on lessons learned from incidents and changing threat landscapes.

Security in the DevOps pipeline is a proactive approach to protecting your organization's software and infrastructure. By embedding security into every stage of the DevOps lifecycle, you can identify and address vulnerabilities early, reduce security risks, and maintain a secure and resilient software delivery process. Ultimately, DevSecOps empowers teams to deliver secure applications with confidence and agility.

B. Securing Containers and Container Orchestration: Protecting the Heart of DevOps

Containers and container orchestration platforms like Docker and Kubernetes have become integral to modern DevOps practices, enabling the rapid deployment and scaling of applications. However, ensuring the security of containerized environments is a paramount concern. In this in-depth exploration, we'll delve into the key principles, best practices, and strategies for securing containers and container orchestration, safeguarding your applications and data in the DevOps ecosystem.

Principles of Container Security:

1. **Immutable Infrastructure:** Containers should be treated as disposable and immutable. Once created, containers should not be modified; instead, new, patched containers should replace them. This approach minimizes the risk of configuration drift and vulnerabilities.

2. **Defense in Depth:** Apply a multi-layered security approach. Protect not only the containers themselves but also the container host, the container registry, and the orchestration platform. Multiple layers of security provide redundancy and resilience.

3. **Least Privilege:** Employ the principle of least privilege for containerized applications and processes. Containers should only have access to the resources and permissions necessary for their intended function.

4. **Continuous Monitoring:** Implement continuous monitoring of containerized environments, including runtime behavior, network traffic, and security events. Real-time alerts and auditing are essential for threat detection and response.

Best Practices for Securing Containers:

1. **Image Security:**

    • **Use Trusted Base Images:** Start with trusted and

official base images from well-known sources like Docker Hub. Verify image integrity and signatures.

- **Scan for Vulnerabilities:** Regularly scan container images for known vulnerabilities using tools like Clair, Trivy, or container security platforms.

- **Regularly Update Images:** Keep container images up to date by regularly rebuilding them with updated software and security patches.

2. **Container Runtime Security:**

- **Isolation:** Implement strong container isolation using technologies like Docker's default seccomp profiles and AppArmor/SELinux.

- **Resource Constraints:** Limit container resource usage to prevent resource exhaustion attacks.

- **Runtime Protection:** Use runtime security tools like Falco or Sysdig to monitor container behavior and detect anomalies.

3. **Container Registry Security:**

- **Access Control:** Implement access control and authentication for your container registry. Only authorized users should be able to push and pull images.

- **Content Trust:** Enable content trust to ensure the integrity of images. Use Notary or Docker Content Trust to sign and verify image signatures.

4. **Network Security:**

- **Network Policies:** Define network policies in your container orchestration platform (e.g., Kubernetes Network Policies) to control traffic between containers.

- **Segmentation:** Segment containers into different network zones based on their roles and sensitivity.

Best Practices for Securing Container Orchestration:

1. **Cluster Security:**

- **Control Plane Access:** Secure access to the control plane of your orchestration platform. Use strong authentication and authorization mechanisms.

- **Node Security:** Protect worker nodes from unauthorized access and ensure they are regularly patched and updated.

2. **API Security:**

- **API Access Control:** Secure the orchestration API, and limit API access to authorized users and services.

- **API Authentication:** Use mutual TLS (mTLS) authentication for API communication to verify the identity of clients.

3. **Secrets Management:**

- **Secrets Encryption:** Encrypt sensitive data, such as secrets and configuration files, at rest and in transit.

- **Secrets Vault:** Use dedicated secrets management solutions like HashiCorp Vault to store and distribute secrets securely.

4. **Pod and Container Security:**

- **Pod Security Policies:** Define and enforce pod security policies to control the security posture of pods running in your cluster.

- **Runtime Sandboxing:** Utilize runtime sandboxes like gVisor or Kata Containers for additional isolation.

5. **Monitoring and Logging:**

- **Centralized Logging:** Aggregate logs from containers

and orchestration platform components for analysis and audit.

- **Security Events:** Continuously monitor for security events, such as unauthorized access or suspicious container behavior.

Securing containers and container orchestration is an ongoing process that requires vigilance and a proactive approach. By adhering to these best practices and principles, organizations can reduce the attack surface, detect and respond to security incidents more effectively, and maintain a robust security posture in their DevOps environments. Ultimately, this approach ensures that the benefits of containerization and orchestration are realized without compromising security.

C. Identity and Access Management (IAM): Safeguarding DevOps Environments

Identity and Access Management (IAM) plays a crucial role in securing DevOps environments. IAM refers to the practices, processes, and technologies used to manage and control access to resources and systems. In the context of DevOps, IAM helps ensure that only authorized individuals and services can access and modify critical infrastructure and application components. In this in-depth exploration, we will delve into the principles, best practices, and key considerations for implementing effective IAM in DevOps.

Principles of IAM in DevOps:

1. **Principle of Least Privilege (PoLP):** IAM follows the PoLP, which means that individuals and services are granted only the minimum level of access required to perform their tasks. This principle limits the potential damage that can be caused by compromised credentials.

2. **Access Control:** IAM enforces access controls based on roles, permissions, and policies. Access control lists (ACLs) and role-based access control (RBAC) are commonly used mechanisms to define who can access resources.

3. **Authentication and Authorization:** IAM ensures that users and services are authenticated and authorized correctly. Authentication verifies the identity of users or services, while authorization determines what actions they are allowed to perform.

4. **Multi-Factor Authentication (MFA):** To enhance security, IAM often incorporates MFA, requiring users to provide multiple forms of authentication before granting access. This adds an extra layer of protection against unauthorized access.

5. **Auditing and Logging:** IAM includes auditing and logging capabilities to track access and changes to resources. Audit

logs are crucial for identifying security incidents and maintaining compliance.

IAM Best Practices in DevOps:

1. **Centralized Identity Management:**

   - Use a centralized identity provider (IdP) such as Active Directory, LDAP, or cloud-based solutions like AWS IAM or Azure Active Directory. Centralized identity management simplifies user provisioning and deprovisioning.

2. **Roles and Groups:**

   - Organize users and services into roles and groups based on their responsibilities and permissions. This streamlines access control and reduces administrative overhead.

3. **Implement Strong Authentication:**

   - Enforce strong authentication mechanisms, such as MFA, for all users and services that access DevOps resources.

4. **Immutable Infrastructure:**

   - Implement IAM policies as code (IaC) to ensure that access controls are applied consistently to infrastructure and applications. Tools like Terraform or AWS CloudFormation can help with IaC.

5. **Least Privilege Access:**

   - Apply the principle of least privilege rigorously. Review and update permissions regularly to ensure users and services have only the necessary access.

6. **Role-Based Access Control (RBAC):**

   - Implement RBAC to assign permissions to roles rather than individual users. This simplifies access management and reduces the risk of errors.

7. **Audit Trails and Monitoring:**

   - Enable auditing and monitoring of IAM activities. Use tools like AWS CloudTrail or Azure Monitor to log IAM events and detect suspicious activities.

   IAM for Service Accounts and Containers:

IAM in DevOps also extends to service accounts and containers:

1. **Service Accounts:** Service accounts for applications and services should have their own credentials and permissions. Avoid using personal user accounts for automated processes.

2. **Container Access:** Secure access to containers by using service-specific identities and secrets management tools. Kubernetes, for example, provides service accounts for this purpose.

IAM Challenges in DevOps:

Implementing IAM in DevOps environments can present certain challenges:

1. **Complexity:** Managing access controls and permissions for a dynamic, containerized environment can be complex. Automation and clear policies are essential to maintaining control.

2. **Scalability:** As DevOps environments scale, IAM management becomes more challenging. IAM solutions must be capable of handling a growing number of users, services, and resources.

3. **Visibility:** It can be challenging to maintain visibility into IAM activities and security events across a distributed DevOps environment. Centralized monitoring and alerting are critical.

4. **Securing Secrets:** Managing and securing secrets, API keys, and other sensitive information used by applications and services is crucial. Tools like HashiCorp Vault or AWS Secrets Manager can help.

In conclusion, IAM is a cornerstone of DevOps security, ensuring that only authorized users and services have access to critical resources. By adhering to IAM principles and best practices, organizations can build robust and secure DevOps pipelines while minimizing the risk of unauthorized access and data breaches. IAM should be an integral part of any DevOps security strategy, enabling teams to achieve the delicate balance between speed and security.

D. Compliance as Code: Automating Regulatory and Security Compliance in DevOps

Compliance as Code (CaaC) is an emerging practice in DevOps that combines the principles of infrastructure as code (IaC) with regulatory and security compliance requirements. It aims to automate and integrate compliance checks and controls into the DevOps pipeline, ensuring that applications and infrastructure adhere to organizational, regulatory, and security standards. In this in-depth exploration, we will delve into the principles, benefits, and best practices of Compliance as Code and its pivotal role in DevOps.

Principles of Compliance as Code:

1. **Automation:** CaaC emphasizes automation as the primary means of enforcing compliance. Compliance checks and

controls are codified and integrated into the DevOps pipeline, eliminating manual intervention and the risk of human error.

2. **Policy as Code:** Compliance policies, including security, regulatory, and organizational standards, are expressed in code form. This code defines what is considered compliant and provides a clear, automated way to evaluate compliance.

3. **Continuous Compliance:** CaaC ensures that compliance checks are continuous and integrated into the DevOps workflow. Compliance is assessed at every stage of the development and deployment process, not just as a one-time event.

4. **Feedback Loop:** Compliance violations trigger feedback loops that notify relevant stakeholders and initiate remediation actions automatically. This enables rapid response and correction of compliance issues.

Benefits of Compliance as Code:

1. **Consistency:** CaaC ensures that compliance checks are consistent and applied uniformly across all environments, reducing the risk of configuration drift between development, testing, and production.

2. **Efficiency:** Automation streamlines compliance assessments, reducing the time and effort required for manual audits and

checks. This allows teams to focus on more strategic tasks.

3. **Agility:** By integrating compliance into the DevOps pipeline, organizations can confidently release code faster, knowing that it adheres to compliance standards. This aligns with the principles of DevOps.

4. **Risk Mitigation:** CaaC helps identify compliance issues early in the development process, reducing the potential impact of non-compliance and security vulnerabilities.

Best Practices for Implementing Compliance as Code:

1. **Define Compliance Policies:**

   - Start by defining clear and comprehensive compliance policies. These policies should cover regulatory requirements, security standards, and organizational guidelines.

2. **Express Policies as Code:**

   - Translate compliance policies into code form using a domain-specific language or a scripting language. Tools like Open Policy Agent (OPA) or HashiCorp Sentinel are commonly used for this purpose.

3. **Integrate with CI/CD Pipelines:**

   - Incorporate compliance checks into your CI/CD

pipelines. Implement pre-deployment checks to ensure that code and infrastructure comply with policies before deployment.

4. **Automate Remediation:**

   - Implement automated remediation actions that correct compliance violations when they are detected. This might include rolling back changes or adjusting configurations.

5. **Implement Version Control:**

   - Store compliance policies as code in version control systems. This ensures that policies can be tracked, reviewed, and updated like any other codebase.

6. **Logging and Auditing:**

   - Maintain logs and audit trails of compliance assessments and remediation actions. This is crucial for compliance reporting and auditing.

7. **Monitoring and Alerting:**

   - Set up monitoring and alerting systems to notify teams of compliance violations in real-time. This enables rapid response and remediation.

8. **Training and Documentation:**

- Ensure that teams are trained in CaaC practices and that documentation is available to guide developers and operations staff in compliance procedures.

Challenges of Compliance as Code:

Implementing Compliance as Code may pose certain challenges:

1. **Complexity:** Managing compliance policies in code can be complex, especially for organizations with extensive regulatory requirements.

2. **Integration:** Integrating compliance checks into existing CI/CD pipelines and workflows may require significant effort and coordination.

3. **Change Management:** Updating compliance policies and code as regulations change or evolve can be challenging. Organizations must have processes in place for managing these changes effectively.

4. **Tool Selection:** Choosing the right tools and frameworks for expressing and enforcing compliance policies is crucial.

Compliance as Code is a powerful approach for ensuring that applications and infrastructure adhere to regulatory and security standards in the fast-paced world of DevOps. By codifying compliance policies, automating assessments, and integrating checks into the DevOps pipeline, organizations can achieve continuous compliance, reduce risks, and streamline compliance management, ultimately aligning security and compliance with DevOps principles.

E. DevSecOps Practices: Integrating Security Throughout the DevOps Lifecycle

DevSecOps is a philosophy and set of practices that emphasizes the integration of security into every phase of the DevOps lifecycle. It extends the principles of DevOps, which prioritize collaboration, automation, and rapid software delivery, to include security considerations. In this in-depth exploration, we'll delve into the principles, practices, and key components of DevSecOps, highlighting its importance in ensuring the security and resilience of modern software systems.

Key Principles of DevSecOps:

1. **Shift Left:** The fundamental principle of DevSecOps is to "shift left" security by addressing it as early as possible in the software development lifecycle. This means that security considerations are integrated into the design, coding, and testing phases, rather than being treated as a separate, post-development activity.

2. **Automation:** Automation is a core tenet of DevSecOps. Security checks, such as vulnerability scanning, code analysis, and compliance assessments, are automated and integrated into CI/CD pipelines. Automated security tests are run consistently and rapidly, reducing the time required to identify and remediate security issues.

3. **Collaboration:** DevSecOps fosters collaboration among development, operations, and security teams. Cross-functional teams work together to define security requirements, develop secure code, and ensure that security is maintained throughout the software delivery process.

4. **Continuous Monitoring:** Continuous monitoring and feedback are essential components of DevSecOps. Systems are monitored for security threats and vulnerabilities in real-time, and feedback loops provide timely information to development and operations teams for remediation.

DevSecOps Practices and Strategies:

1. **Secure Coding Standards:** Establish and enforce secure coding standards and best practices. Tools like static code analyzers and linters can help identify security vulnerabilities during development.

2. **Automated Security Testing:** Integrate automated security testing into the CI/CD pipeline. This includes static

application security testing (SAST), dynamic application security testing (DAST), and software composition analysis (SCA) to identify vulnerabilities in code and dependencies.

3. **Infrastructure as Code (IaC) Security:** Apply security checks and controls to infrastructure code using IaC practices. Tools like Terraform, Ansible, or AWS CloudFormation can be used to define secure infrastructure configurations.

4. **Container Security:** Implement container security practices, such as scanning container images for vulnerabilities, enforcing runtime security policies, and securely managing secrets and credentials used in containers.

5. **Vulnerability Management:** Develop a vulnerability management program that includes regular scanning and assessment of software components, libraries, and dependencies. Prioritize and remediate vulnerabilities based on their severity and potential impact.

6. **Access Control and Identity Management:** Implement strong access controls, identity and access management (IAM) policies, and role-based access control (RBAC) to limit access to systems and resources based on the principle of least privilege.

7. **Security Information and Event Management (SIEM):** Utilize SIEM tools to collect and analyze security event data

from various sources. SIEM systems help detect and respond to security incidents in real-time.

8. **Incident Response:** Develop and test incident response plans that outline the steps to take in the event of a security incident. Ensure that teams are prepared to respond effectively to security breaches.

9. **Compliance Automation:** Automate compliance checks to ensure that systems adhere to regulatory and security standards. Compliance as code (CaaC) practices can help codify and enforce compliance requirements.

10. **Security Training and Awareness:** Provide security training and awareness programs for development and operations teams. Security champions or advocates can help promote security knowledge and practices within teams.

Challenges of DevSecOps:

1. **Cultural Shift:** Implementing DevSecOps often requires a cultural shift within organizations to break down silos between development, operations, and security teams.

2. **Tool Integration:** Integrating security tools into existing DevOps workflows can be challenging and may require adjustments to CI/CD pipelines.

3. **Skills Gap:** Teams may require training and upskilling in

security practices and tools to effectively implement DevSecOps.

4. **Complexity:** Managing the complexity of security controls, policies, and compliance requirements in a DevSecOps environment can be demanding.

DevSecOps is not a one-time implementation but an ongoing commitment to integrating security into the DevOps lifecycle. By adhering to the principles and practices of DevSecOps, organizations can enhance the security posture of their software systems while maintaining agility and speed in software development and delivery. Ultimately, DevSecOps helps strike a balance between innovation, security, and compliance in today's fast-paced digital landscape.

CHAPTER 8

Continuous Monitoring and Feedback

Continuous Monitoring and Feedback is a critical practice within DevOps that focuses on maintaining a real-time, comprehensive view of the performance, security, and health of software systems and infrastructure. It goes beyond traditional monitoring approaches by providing ongoing insights and actionable feedback to development, operations, and security teams. In this introductory exploration, we'll delve into the fundamental concepts, benefits, and significance of Continuous Monitoring and Feedback in the context of DevOps.

A. The Importance of Monitoring in DevOps: Ensuring Performance, Reliability, and Security

Monitoring is a cornerstone of DevOps practices, playing a pivotal role in ensuring the performance, reliability, and security of software systems and infrastructure. In the DevOps philosophy, monitoring goes beyond traditional IT operations by becoming an integral part of the development lifecycle. It provides real-time visibility into the health and behavior of applications, services, and the underlying infrastructure, allowing teams to proactively identify issues, optimize performance, and maintain a robust, resilient ecosystem. In this in-depth exploration, we'll delve into the critical importance of monitoring in DevOps and its multifaceted benefits.

1. Early Issue Detection and Resolution:

Monitoring provides early warning signs of potential issues, allowing teams to detect and address problems before they escalate. This proactive approach reduces downtime, enhances system stability, and minimizes the impact on users.

2. Improved Performance Optimization:

Continuous monitoring enables performance tuning and optimization. Teams can identify bottlenecks, resource constraints, and inefficient code or configurations, leading to better application performance and resource utilization.

3. Enhanced Reliability and Availability:

Reliability is a core DevOps principle, and monitoring is instrumental in achieving it. By tracking system reliability metrics and uptime, teams can ensure that applications are available and responsive to users at all times.

4. Security and Compliance:

Monitoring plays a crucial role in security and compliance

efforts. Security monitoring helps detect and respond to suspicious activities, while compliance monitoring ensures that systems adhere to regulatory standards and internal policies.

5. Rapid Issue Resolution:

Monitoring tools provide real-time data, enabling rapid root cause analysis and issue resolution. This reduces mean time to resolution (MTTR) and minimizes the impact on end-users.

6. Scalability and Resource Management:

As applications and infrastructure scale dynamically, monitoring helps manage resource allocation and scalability. Teams can ensure that resources are provisioned and de-provisioned as needed, optimizing costs and performance.

7. Continuous Feedback Loops:

Monitoring generates data and metrics that feed into feedback loops within the DevOps cycle. This feedback informs development and operational decisions, fostering a culture of continuous improvement.

8. Predictive Analysis:

Advanced monitoring systems can use machine learning and predictive analytics to forecast potential issues or resource needs. This allows teams to be proactive in addressing upcoming challenges.

9. Infrastructure as Code (IaC) Integration:

Monitoring can be integrated into IaC practices, ensuring that infrastructure configurations align with desired performance and security standards. Infrastructure changes can trigger automatic monitoring setup.

10. User Experience Optimization:

Monitoring helps gauge user experience by tracking response times, error rates, and user behavior. This insight is valuable for user-centric application design and performance improvements.

11. Compliance and Audit Trails:

For organizations subject to regulatory requirements, monitoring provides audit trails and logs necessary for compliance reporting and security audits.

12. Cost Efficiency:

Monitoring helps optimize resource usage, reducing unnecessary costs associated with over-provisioning or inefficient resource allocation.

Challenges of Monitoring in DevOps:

While monitoring is crucial in DevOps, it comes with its

challenges:

1. **Tool Complexity:** Choosing and implementing monitoring tools can be complex, as there are various options available for different use cases.

2. **Data Overload:** Collecting vast amounts of data can lead to information overload. Teams must define meaningful metrics and alerts to focus on relevant data.

3. **Alert Fatigue:** Excessive alerts can lead to alert fatigue, where teams become desensitized to alerts. Fine-tuning alerting rules is essential to avoid this issue.

4. **Resource Consumption:** Monitoring systems themselves consume resources, and improper monitoring can introduce performance overhead.

In conclusion, monitoring is an integral part of DevOps, providing essential insights into system performance, security, and reliability. It empowers teams to proactively address issues, optimize resources, and continuously improve software delivery. As DevOps practices continue to evolve, monitoring remains a fundamental practice for ensuring the delivery of high-quality, reliable, and secure applications and services.

B. Metrics and Key Performance Indicators (KPIs) in DevOps: Measuring Success and Driving Continuous Improvement

Metrics and Key Performance Indicators (KPIs) are essential components of any successful DevOps practice. They provide quantifiable, objective insights into various aspects of the software development and delivery process, helping teams make data-driven decisions, identify areas for improvement, and measure the success of their DevOps initiatives. In this in-depth exploration, we'll delve into the significance of metrics and KPIs in DevOps, their role in driving continuous improvement, and examples of metrics across different DevOps stages.

Understanding Metrics and KPIs:

- **Metrics:** Metrics are quantifiable measurements that track various aspects of a process, system, or application. In DevOps, metrics can include performance data, error rates, resource utilization, and more. They provide a snapshot of the current state of a system or process.

- **Key Performance Indicators (KPIs):** KPIs are a subset of metrics that are strategically chosen to represent critical aspects of a project, process, or system. They help organizations gauge progress toward specific goals and objectives.

The Significance of Metrics and KPIs in DevOps:

1. **Data-Driven Decision Making:** Metrics and KPIs provide objective data that guides decision-making. Teams can use this information to identify bottlenecks, allocate resources effectively, and prioritize tasks based on their impact on business objectives.

2. **Continuous Improvement:** DevOps encourages a culture of continuous improvement, and metrics are central to this philosophy. Teams can track their performance over time, identify trends, and iteratively refine processes to enhance efficiency and quality.

3. **Performance Monitoring:** Metrics help teams monitor the performance of applications and infrastructure in real-time. This allows for proactive issue detection and resolution, reducing downtime and improving user experience.

4. **Predictive Analysis:** Historical metrics data can be used to make predictions about future performance and resource needs. This enables proactive planning for scalability and resource allocation.

5. **Communication and Transparency:** Metrics provide a common language for communication among cross-functional DevOps teams. They offer a clear, objective way to convey the status of projects and systems to stakeholders.

Examples of Metrics and KPIs in DevOps:

1. **Deployment Frequency:** Measures how often new code changes are deployed to production. High deployment frequency is often associated with mature DevOps practices.

2. **Lead Time for Changes:** The time it takes for code changes to move from development to production. A shorter lead time indicates efficient processes.

3. **Change Failure Rate:** The percentage of code changes that result in failures or defects. Lower change failure rates indicate better code quality and testing practices.

4. **Mean Time to Recovery (MTTR):** The average time it takes to recover from a system failure or incident. Lower MTTR indicates effective incident response and resolution processes.

5. **Code Coverage:** Measures the percentage of code covered by automated tests. Higher code coverage indicates better test coverage and potentially fewer defects in production.

6. **Resource Utilization:** Monitors the utilization of CPU, memory, storage, and other resources in the infrastructure. Efficient resource utilization reduces costs and improves performance.

7. **Error Rates:** Tracks the frequency and severity of errors or exceptions in an application. Low error rates are indicative of

stable and reliable software.

8. **User Satisfaction:** Collects user feedback and surveys to measure satisfaction with the application's performance and features.

9. **Security Vulnerabilities:** Counts the number of security vulnerabilities and their severity level. Lower vulnerability counts and lower severity indicate stronger security practices.

Challenges and Considerations:

While metrics and KPIs are invaluable in DevOps, there are challenges to consider:

1. **Choosing the Right Metrics:** Selecting meaningful and relevant metrics is crucial. Metrics should align with business objectives and provide actionable insights.

2. **Data Quality:** Accurate and reliable data is essential. Poor data quality can lead to incorrect conclusions and decisions.

3. **Context Matters:** Metrics should be interpreted in the context of the specific environment and goals. What's considered a "good" metric value may vary between organizations and projects.

4. **Avoiding Vanity Metrics:** Beware of metrics that look good on paper but don't reflect the actual health or performance of

the system.

In conclusion, metrics and KPIs are integral to DevOps practices, enabling organizations to measure progress, identify areas for improvement, and make data-driven decisions. By tracking the right metrics and focusing on KPIs that align with business goals, DevOps teams can continuously enhance their processes, optimize performance, and deliver high-quality software efficiently.

C. Log Management and Analysis in DevOps: Harnessing Data for Insights and Security

Log management and analysis are fundamental practices within DevOps that involve collecting, storing, and analyzing log data generated by software applications, infrastructure components, and systems. Logs are records of events and actions that occur within these environments, and effective log management and analysis provide valuable insights into system behavior, performance, and security. In this in-depth exploration, we'll delve into the significance of log management and analysis in DevOps, the key components, best practices, and tools involved, as well as the benefits of this practice.

The Significance of Log Management and Analysis in DevOps:

1. **Visibility and Troubleshooting:** Logs offer visibility into the inner workings of systems, applications, and services. When issues arise, logs become indispensable for diagnosing and troubleshooting problems, reducing mean time to resolution (MTTR).

2. **Performance Monitoring:** Logs contain data on system performance, resource utilization, and response times. Analyzing this information helps teams identify bottlenecks, optimize resource allocation, and enhance application performance.

3. **Security Monitoring:** Logs play a crucial role in security by recording potentially suspicious activities, unauthorized access attempts, and security events. Security teams can use log analysis to detect and respond to threats in real-time.

4. **Compliance and Audit Trails:** Many industries and organizations require compliance with specific regulations. Log management ensures that detailed records are available for auditing and compliance reporting.

5. **Capacity Planning:** By tracking resource usage and system behavior over time, logs aid in capacity planning. This enables teams to anticipate and meet resource requirements as systems

scale.

Key Components of Log Management and Analysis:

1. **Log Collection:** The first step is collecting log data from various sources, including servers, applications, network devices, and security tools. This often involves deploying log agents or integrating with logging APIs.

2. **Log Storage:** Logs must be stored in a centralized and scalable repository. Common options include log management platforms, cloud-based storage, or on-premises solutions.

3. **Log Parsing and Normalization:** Logs are often generated in different formats and structures. Parsing and normalization processes extract relevant information and make logs consistent for analysis.

4. **Indexing and Search:** Indexing enables efficient searching and retrieval of log data. It allows teams to quickly locate specific log entries or patterns within large log datasets.

5. **Analysis and Alerting:** Log analysis tools help identify trends, anomalies, and potential issues. Alerting mechanisms notify teams in real-time when predefined conditions or thresholds are met.

6. **Retention and Archiving:** Logs should be retained based on organizational policies and compliance requirements. Long-

term archiving may be necessary to meet regulatory standards.

7. **Visualization and Reporting:** Log data is often visualized through dashboards and reports, providing an at-a-glance view of system health and performance.

Best Practices in Log Management and Analysis:

1. **Centralized Logging:** Centralize log data from all sources to simplify management and analysis.

2. **Standardized Logging Formats:** Ensure that logs follow standardized formats and include essential metadata for easy parsing and analysis.

3. **Retention Policies:** Define log retention policies to balance storage costs with compliance and troubleshooting needs.

4. **Security Controls:** Implement security controls to protect log data from unauthorized access and tampering.

5. **Automated Alerts:** Set up automated alerts for critical events or unusual activity to enable proactive response.

6. **Regular Review and Analysis:** Periodically review log data to identify trends, areas for optimization, and potential security threats.

Log Management and Analysis Tools:

1. **ELK Stack (Elasticsearch, Logstash, Kibana):** An open-source solution for log management, it includes Elasticsearch for indexing and searching, Logstash for data collection and parsing, and Kibana for visualization.

2. **Splunk:** A popular commercial log management and analysis platform that offers powerful search and visualization capabilities.

3. **Graylog:** An open-source log management and analysis platform that provides centralized logging and robust alerting features.

4. **Sumo Logic:** A cloud-based log management and analysis service that offers real-time monitoring, alerting, and analytics.

5. **AWS CloudWatch Logs:** Amazon's log management service for AWS environments, providing log storage, analysis, and integration with other AWS services.

Benefits of Log Management and Analysis in DevOps:

1. **Rapid Issue Resolution:** Logs enable quick identification and resolution of issues, reducing downtime and enhancing user experience.

2. **Improved Security:** Log analysis helps detect security threats and suspicious activities in real-time, enhancing overall system security.

3. **Performance Optimization:** Monitoring and analyzing logs enable teams to optimize resource allocation and improve application performance.

4. **Compliance and Auditing:** Proper log management ensures compliance with regulatory requirements and provides audit trails for reporting.

5. **Capacity Planning:** Log data aids in forecasting and planning for resource scalability.

In conclusion, log management and analysis are indispensable practices within DevOps, offering insights into system performance, security, and compliance. By collecting, storing, and analyzing log data effectively, DevOps teams can streamline issue resolution, enhance security, optimize performance, and maintain robust, reliable systems.

D. Feedback Loops for Continuous Improvement in DevOps: Closing the Loop for Excellence

Feedback loops are an integral part of DevOps, facilitating continuous improvement by gathering insights, evaluating performance, and driving informed decisions. These loops help teams adapt, refine processes, and enhance software quality in a dynamic and agile environment. In this in-depth exploration, we'll delve into the significance of feedback loops in DevOps, their key types, and best practices for leveraging them to achieve continuous improvement.

The Significance of Feedback Loops in DevOps:

Feedback loops in DevOps serve several critical purposes:

1. **Continuous Learning:** They enable teams to learn from past experiences, both successes and failures, fostering a culture of learning and adaptation.

2. **Visibility:** Feedback loops provide visibility into system behavior, application performance, and user experience, offering data-driven insights.

3. **Issue Detection:** Rapid feedback helps teams detect issues and defects early in the development process, reducing the cost and effort required for remediation.

4. **Alignment with Business Goals:** Feedback loops align development and operational activities with broader business objectives, ensuring that teams prioritize work that delivers value to the organization.

Key Types of Feedback Loops in DevOps:

1. **Development Feedback Loop:**

   - **Automated Testing:** Continuous integration (CI) pipelines include automated testing stages, such as unit tests, integration tests, and acceptance tests. Feedback from these tests helps developers identify and address issues in code.

   - **Code Reviews:** Peer code reviews provide feedback on code quality, design, and adherence to coding standards.

   - **Static Code Analysis:** Tools like static code analyzers automatically identify code quality issues, security vulnerabilities, and potential bugs.

2. **Operations Feedback Loop:**

   - **Monitoring and Alerting:** Real-time monitoring of applications and infrastructure generates alerts when issues or anomalies are detected, enabling rapid response.

   - **Incident Management:** When incidents occur, the incident response process collects feedback on what went wrong and how to prevent similar incidents in the future.

- **Change Management:** Feedback on the impact of changes and deployments helps teams assess the success of changes and evaluate the effectiveness of rollback procedures.

3. **User Feedback Loop:**

   - **User Experience (UX) Monitoring:** Tools and analytics gather data on user behavior, allowing organizations to understand how users interact with applications and identify areas for improvement.

   - **User Surveys and Feedback:** Collecting user feedback through surveys and direct communication provides insights into user satisfaction and feature requests.

4. **Business Feedback Loop:**

   - **Key Performance Indicators (KPIs):** Business-level KPIs, such as revenue, customer acquisition, and user retention, provide feedback on the overall success of software products and services.

   - **Market Research:** Feedback from market research and competitive analysis informs strategic decisions and product direction.

Best Practices for Effective Feedback Loops:

1. **Automate Where Possible:** Implement automated testing, monitoring, and alerting to provide immediate feedback. Automated tools offer consistency and speed.

2. **Define Clear Objectives:** Clearly define the objectives and goals of each feedback loop to ensure that the feedback collected aligns with the desired outcomes.

3. **Continuous Feedback:** Establish a culture of continuous feedback collection and analysis rather than relying on periodic assessments.

4. **Feedback Analysis:** Develop processes for analyzing feedback data, identifying trends, and prioritizing improvements.

5. **Cross-Functional Collaboration:** Foster collaboration between development, operations, and business teams to ensure a holistic view of feedback.

6. **Closed-Loop Actions:** Ensure that feedback leads to actionable improvements. Define and track corrective actions based on feedback.

7. **Iterative Improvement:** Use feedback to drive iterative improvements in processes, systems, and products.

Challenges and Considerations:

1. **Data Overload:** Collecting large amounts of feedback data can lead to information overload. Tools for data analysis and visualization are essential.

2. **Cultural Resistance:** Some organizations may face resistance to feedback-driven changes. Encourage a culture of openness to feedback and continuous improvement.

3. **Integration Complexity:** Integrating feedback mechanisms into existing processes and systems may be challenging and require careful planning.

In conclusion, feedback loops are the lifeblood of continuous improvement in DevOps. They provide valuable insights, drive informed decision-making, and enable teams to adapt and excel in a rapidly evolving environment. By establishing effective feedback mechanisms and incorporating feedback-driven improvements into their practices, DevOps teams can deliver higher-quality software, enhance operational efficiency, and align their efforts with the overarching goals of the organization.

CHAPTER 9

DevOps in the Cloud

DevOps practices have undergone a significant transformation with the advent of cloud computing. DevOps in the cloud represents a convergence of methodologies and technologies that leverage the scalability, agility, and automation capabilities offered by cloud platforms. In this introductory exploration, we'll embark on a journey to understand the synergy between DevOps and the cloud, the advantages it brings, and how organizations can harness this combination to accelerate their software development and delivery processes.

A. Cloud Services and DevOps: The Synergy that Drives Innovation

The marriage of cloud services and DevOps has fundamentally transformed the landscape of software development and operations. DevOps practices, which emphasize collaboration, automation, and continuous improvement, are greatly empowered by the capabilities offered by cloud computing. In this in-depth exploration, we'll delve into the profound impact of cloud services on DevOps, the key benefits it brings, and the ways in which organizations can harness this synergy for innovation and efficiency.

1. On-Demand Scalability:

One of the most compelling aspects of cloud services for DevOps is the ability to scale resources on-demand. Cloud providers offer elastic infrastructure, allowing organizations to quickly provision and de-provision computing resources as needed. This scalability aligns seamlessly with DevOps principles, enabling teams to respond to varying workloads and deploy applications more efficiently. Autoscaling, a common practice in DevOps, is made easier with cloud services as it dynamically adjusts resources based on application demand.

2. Infrastructure as Code (IaC):

DevOps promotes the use of Infrastructure as Code (IaC) to define and provision infrastructure resources. Cloud services provide a natural environment for IaC tools like Terraform and AWS CloudFormation, allowing teams to codify and version-control infrastructure configurations. This ensures that infrastructure is consistent, reproducible, and can be easily managed alongside application code.

3. Automation and Orchestration:

Cloud services offer extensive automation capabilities, allowing DevOps teams to automate deployment pipelines, configuration management, and scaling operations. Orchestrating these tasks in the cloud streamlines the DevOps workflow, reduces manual intervention, and accelerates software delivery. Tools like AWS Lambda and Azure Functions enable serverless computing, further automating resource management.

4. DevOps Tools Integration:

Cloud providers offer integrations with popular DevOps tools, such as Jenkins, GitLab CI/CD, and Kubernetes. This integration simplifies the deployment and management of these tools, promoting a consistent and efficient DevOps toolchain.

5. Collaboration and Remote Work:

Cloud services facilitate collaboration among geographically distributed DevOps teams. Teams can access development and testing environments from anywhere, fostering remote work capabilities. Cloud-based collaboration tools like Slack, Microsoft Teams, and Jira enhance communication and coordination.

6. Managed Services:

Cloud providers offer a wide range of managed services, including databases, container orchestration, and machine learning. Leveraging these managed services allows DevOps teams to offload operational overhead, focus on application development, and benefit from built-in scalability and reliability.

7. Disaster Recovery and High Availability:

Cloud services provide built-in disaster recovery and high availability options. DevOps teams can design and implement resilient architectures using cloud features like multi-region redundancy, automated backups, and failover mechanisms.

8. Cost Optimization:

Cloud services offer cost optimization tools and practices that align with DevOps principles. Teams can use cost monitoring, budgeting, and optimization services to control expenses and ensure efficient resource utilization.

Challenges and Considerations:

While the marriage of cloud services and DevOps is transformative, it comes with challenges:

1. **Security and Compliance:** DevOps teams must ensure that cloud configurations adhere to security and compliance standards. Cloud security tools and best practices are essential.

2. **Cost Management:** Cloud costs can escalate if not managed properly. Teams should implement cost control measures and regularly analyze spending.

3. **Vendor Lock-In:** Organizations may face vendor lock-in concerns when relying heavily on a single cloud provider's

services. Strategies for multi-cloud or hybrid cloud deployments should be considered.

4. **Complexity:** The sheer number of cloud services and options can be overwhelming. Teams need to balance the adoption of new services with simplicity and manageability.

In conclusion, cloud services and DevOps are intertwined, offering a powerful combination for organizations striving to innovate, scale, and accelerate their software development and delivery processes. By embracing cloud-native DevOps practices, teams can harness the agility, automation, and scalability of the cloud to drive efficiency, resilience, and competitiveness in today's dynamic digital landscape.

B. Serverless Computing and DevOps: A Paradigm Shift in Application Deployment

Serverless computing, often referred to as Function as a Service (FaaS), represents a paradigm shift in how applications are developed, deployed, and scaled. This innovative approach has significant implications for DevOps practices, offering new opportunities and challenges. In this in-depth exploration, we'll delve into the intersection of serverless computing and DevOps, exploring the key concepts, benefits, best practices, and considerations for effectively integrating serverless into your DevOps workflow.

1. Key Concepts of Serverless Computing:

- **Event-Driven Execution:** Serverless functions are triggered by events, such as HTTP requests, database changes, or file uploads. They execute in response to these events and automatically scale to handle varying workloads.

- **Stateless Functions:** Serverless functions are stateless, meaning they don't maintain persistent server instances. Each execution is isolated, and there is no need to manage server infrastructure.

- **Pay-as-You-Go Pricing:** Serverless platforms charge based on the actual execution time and resource usage of functions, rather than pre-allocated infrastructure. This aligns with the cost-efficiency aspect of DevOps.

2. Benefits of Serverless Computing for DevOps:

- **Scalability:** Serverless platforms handle automatic scaling, making it easier to handle varying workloads and ensuring optimal resource utilization. This aligns with the DevOps principle of flexibility.

- **Reduced Operational Overhead:** With serverless, there's no need to manage server instances, patching, or infrastructure provisioning, allowing DevOps teams to focus on application code and automation.

- **Rapid Deployment:** Serverless functions can be deployed quickly, reducing the deployment lead time and enabling faster iterations in the DevOps pipeline.

- **Cost-Efficiency:** Serverless platforms offer pay-as-you-go pricing, which can lead to cost savings by eliminating the need to provision and maintain underutilized infrastructure.

3. Best Practices for Serverless and DevOps Integration:

- **Infrastructure as Code (IaC):** Apply IaC practices to define and manage serverless functions, event triggers, and related resources. Tools like AWS SAM (Serverless Application Model) or the Serverless Framework can help.

- **Automated Testing:** Implement automated testing for serverless functions, including unit tests, integration tests, and end-to-end tests. Serverless-specific testing frameworks, like AWS Lambda's AWS SAM Local, can aid in testing locally.

- **Continuous Integration/Continuous Deployment (CI/CD):** Integrate serverless functions into your CI/CD pipeline. Automate the deployment of serverless functions, and ensure proper testing and validation at each stage.

- **Monitoring and Observability:** Use cloud-native monitoring and observability tools to gain insights into the performance and behavior of serverless functions. Services like AWS

CloudWatch and Azure Monitor provide metrics and logs for serverless applications.

- **Security:** Apply security best practices, such as proper access controls and least privilege principles, to serverless functions. Serverless platforms often offer built-in security features for authentication and authorization.

4. Considerations and Challenges:

- **Vendor Lock-In:** Serverless platforms are tied to specific cloud providers, potentially leading to vendor lock-in. Consider strategies for multi-cloud or hybrid deployments if vendor lock-in is a concern.

- **Cold Starts:** Serverless functions may experience "cold starts" with higher initialization times for the first request. Optimize functions and minimize cold start impacts where necessary.

- **Resource Limitations:** Serverless functions have resource limitations, such as execution time and memory. Be aware of these limits and design functions accordingly.

- **Complexity:** Managing serverless functions, event triggers, and dependencies can become complex as applications grow. Use appropriate tools and practices to manage complexity.

In conclusion, serverless computing represents a

transformative shift in application deployment, and its integration with DevOps practices offers numerous benefits. By leveraging serverless functions, DevOps teams can focus on code and application logic while offloading operational concerns to the cloud provider. However, it's essential to understand the unique characteristics and challenges of serverless computing and incorporate best practices to ensure a seamless integration that aligns with the principles of DevOps.

C. Multi-Cloud Strategies in DevOps: Unlocking Flexibility and Resilience

Multi-cloud strategies involve the use of multiple cloud providers to host and manage applications and services. This approach offers significant advantages in terms of flexibility, resilience, and vendor diversification. When integrated with DevOps practices, multi-cloud strategies can empower organizations to optimize their software development and delivery processes. In this in-depth exploration, we'll delve into the world of multi-cloud strategies in DevOps, exploring their benefits, implementation best practices, and considerations.

Benefits of Multi-Cloud Strategies in DevOps:

1. **Vendor Diversification:** Relying on multiple cloud providers reduces the risk of vendor lock-in. Organizations can choose services and pricing models that best fit their needs and

budget.

2. **Geographic Redundancy:** Multi-cloud architectures allow applications to be hosted in geographically diverse regions, improving resilience to regional outages and disasters.

3. **Cost Optimization:** Organizations can take advantage of competitive pricing and cost-effective services from different cloud providers. DevOps teams can select the most cost-efficient provider for each workload.

4. **Service Redundancy:** Leveraging multiple cloud providers ensures that critical services, such as storage, databases, or content delivery, have redundant options, reducing the risk of service disruptions.

5. **Performance Optimization:** Multi-cloud strategies enable organizations to deploy workloads closer to their end-users, reducing latency and improving application performance.

Best Practices for Implementing Multi-Cloud Strategies in DevOps:

1. **Architecture Considerations:**

   - **Design for Portability:** Develop applications and services in a way that makes them easily transferable between cloud providers, using containerization or serverless technologies.

- **Standardize Interfaces:** Standardize interfaces and APIs to abstract the underlying cloud provider, making it easier to switch or use multiple providers.

- **Use Orchestration Tools:** Employ orchestration tools like Kubernetes, which can manage workloads across multiple cloud environments.

2. **Automation and Infrastructure as Code (IaC):**

    - **IaC Compatibility:** Ensure that your infrastructure as code (IaC) scripts and templates are compatible with different cloud providers. Tools like Terraform or AWS Cloud Development Kit (CDK) can assist in this regard.

    - **Automation Scripts:** Automate deployment, scaling, and management tasks to ensure consistent operations across multiple clouds.

3. **Monitoring and Management:**

    - **Unified Monitoring:** Implement unified monitoring and observability solutions that can collect and analyze metrics, logs, and traces from different cloud providers and services.

    - **Centralized Management:** Use management and orchestration tools to centrally manage resources across multiple clouds, making it easier to enforce policies and configurations.

4. **Security and Compliance:**

   - **Consistent Security Policies:** Apply consistent security policies and access controls across all cloud providers to maintain a robust security posture.

   - **Compliance Management:** Ensure compliance with regulatory requirements and industry standards across all cloud environments.

5. **Data Management:**

   - **Data Portability:** Develop data management strategies that allow for easy data migration and synchronization between cloud providers.

   - **Backup and Recovery:** Implement backup and recovery solutions that work seamlessly across multi-cloud environments.

Challenges and Considerations:

1. **Complexity:** Managing resources, configurations, and policies across multiple cloud providers can introduce complexity. DevOps teams must have the skills and tools to manage this complexity effectively.

2. **Cost Management:** While multi-cloud can offer cost advantages, it can also lead to increased complexity in managing and optimizing costs.

3. **Interoperability:** Not all cloud services and features are directly interchangeable between providers. DevOps teams should carefully evaluate which workloads are suitable for multi-cloud deployment.

4. **Data Integration:** Data integration and synchronization between different cloud environments can be challenging. Ensure data consistency and minimize data transfer costs.

5. **Compliance and Security:** Maintaining consistent security and compliance controls across multiple clouds requires careful planning and governance.

In conclusion, multi-cloud strategies in DevOps offer organizations the flexibility and resilience needed to thrive in a dynamic and competitive digital landscape. By carefully designing architectures, automating operations, and managing resources effectively, DevOps teams can harness the power of multiple cloud providers to optimize software development and delivery processes while mitigating risks associated with vendor lock-in and service outages.

D. DevOps Challenges in the Cloud: Navigating the Complexity

DevOps and cloud computing are powerful allies, but the integration of these two domains also introduces unique challenges. As organizations adopt cloud-based infrastructure and services to accelerate their software development and delivery, they must address a range of complexities to ensure success. In this in-depth exploration, we'll examine the key challenges that DevOps teams face when operating in the cloud and explore strategies for overcoming these obstacles.

1. Security and Compliance:

- **Challenge:** Cloud environments often involve a shared responsibility model, where the cloud provider is responsible for securing the underlying infrastructure, while customers are responsible for securing their applications and data. Achieving security and compliance across these shared responsibilities can be complex.

- **Strategy:** DevOps teams must implement robust security practices such as identity and access management (IAM), encryption, and least privilege access. Compliance should be addressed through continuous monitoring and adherence to industry-specific standards and regulations.

2. **Resource Management and Costs:**

- **Challenge:** The cloud offers dynamic scalability, but it can also lead to cost unpredictability if not managed effectively. Overprovisioning and underutilization of resources can result in inflated cloud bills.

- **Strategy:** DevOps teams must implement cost management strategies such as resource tagging, automated scaling, and utilization analysis. Monitoring tools can provide insights into resource usage, helping teams optimize their cloud spending.

3. **Multi-Cloud Complexity:**

- **Challenge:** Organizations adopting multi-cloud strategies face the complexity of managing resources and configurations across different cloud providers. This complexity can lead to challenges in ensuring consistency and avoiding vendor lock-in.

- **Strategy:** Standardize configurations using Infrastructure as Code (IaC) tools that work across multiple cloud providers. Implement centralized management and monitoring solutions to maintain control and visibility.

4. **Data Management and Portability:**

- **Challenge:** Data management becomes complex when data needs to move between on-premises environments and the cloud or between different cloud providers. Ensuring data consistency, availability, and portability can be challenging.

- **Strategy:** Implement data migration and synchronization strategies that align with DevOps practices. Use cloud-native data services and solutions that support multi-cloud data management.

5. Deployment Automation:

- **Challenge:** Orchestrating deployments in the cloud can be complex, especially when dealing with microservices, serverless functions, and distributed architectures. Ensuring consistency and minimizing deployment errors is crucial.

- **Strategy:** Adopt CI/CD (Continuous Integration/Continuous Deployment) pipelines that are cloud-aware. Leverage cloud-native deployment tools and infrastructure automation to ensure reliable and repeatable deployments.

6. Scaling and Performance:

- **Challenge:** While the cloud offers scalability, it also requires DevOps teams to understand and configure auto-scaling and load balancing effectively. Poorly configured scaling can lead to overprovisioning or underperformance.

- **Strategy:** Use monitoring and performance analysis to set appropriate scaling triggers and thresholds. Implement autoscaling policies and regularly test scalability to ensure optimal resource allocation.

7. Vendor Lock-In:

- **Challenge:** Over-reliance on cloud provider-specific services and features can lead to vendor lock-in, making it difficult to migrate workloads to other providers or on-premises environments.

- **Strategy:** Adopt cloud-agnostic practices whenever possible. Standardize on open-source tools and platforms that are compatible with multiple cloud providers. Develop exit strategies to mitigate lock-in risks.

8. Change Management and Cultural Shifts:

- **Challenge:** Transitioning to cloud-based DevOps requires a cultural shift and changes in established processes and workflows. Resistance to change and siloed organizational structures can impede progress.

- **Strategy:** Foster a culture of collaboration, transparency, and continuous learning. Encourage cross-functional teams and provide training and resources to support cultural transformation.

In conclusion, DevOps in the cloud presents both tremendous opportunities and challenges. Addressing these challenges requires a combination of technical solutions, cultural transformation, and a proactive approach to managing cloud resources and configurations. DevOps teams that can effectively navigate these complexities will be well-positioned to leverage the cloud's capabilities and drive innovation in their organizations.

CHAPTER 10

Advanced DevOps Topics

As DevOps continues to evolve, advanced topics emerge that delve deeper into the intricacies and specialized areas of this transformative discipline. In this introductory exploration, we embark on a journey to discover the advanced facets of DevOps, including its applications in microservices architecture, AI and machine learning, chaos engineering, mobile and IoT development, and its unique challenges and solutions when dealing with legacy systems. These advanced topics expand the DevOps landscape, catering to the evolving demands of modern software development and operations.

A. DevOps in Microservices Architecture: Orchestrating Agility and Scale

Microservices architecture has revolutionized the way software is developed and deployed, breaking down monolithic applications into smaller, independently deployable services. DevOps practices play a pivotal role in realizing the potential of microservices, enabling organizations to achieve agility, scalability, and faster time-to-market. In this in-depth exploration, we'll delve into the intricate relationship between DevOps and microservices, examining their core principles, benefits, implementation challenges, and best practices.

1. Key Principles of Microservices Architecture:

- **Decomposition:** Microservices involve breaking down a complex application into smaller, self-contained services that focus on specific business capabilities or functions.

- **Independence:** Each microservice is independently deployable, manageable, and can be developed using different technologies or programming languages.

- **Communication:** Microservices communicate via well-defined APIs or protocols, often over lightweight mechanisms such as HTTP/REST or messaging queues.

- **Scalability:** Microservices can be scaled independently, allowing organizations to allocate resources based on the demand for specific services.

- **Ownership:** Teams are typically responsible for the entire lifecycle of their microservices, from development and testing to deployment and maintenance.

2. Benefits of DevOps in Microservices:

- **Faster Iterations:** DevOps practices enable rapid development, testing, and deployment of microservices, facilitating faster iterations and feature releases.

- **Continuous Integration and Continuous Deployment (CI/CD):** CI/CD pipelines automate the building, testing, and deployment of microservices, ensuring consistent and reliable releases.

- **Scalability:** DevOps practices, including automated scaling, allow microservices to handle varying workloads efficiently.

- **Service Resilience:** DevOps teams can implement robust monitoring, alerting, and self-healing mechanisms to ensure the resilience of microservices in production.

- **Improved Collaboration:** DevOps promotes collaboration between development and operations teams, aligning them to support microservices effectively.

3. Implementation Challenges and Solutions:

- **Service Discovery:** Discovering and managing microservices in dynamic environments can be challenging. Solutions include service registries (e.g., Consul) and API gateways (e.g., Netflix Zuul).

- **Monitoring and Observability:** Ensuring visibility into the performance and behavior of microservices requires comprehensive monitoring and observability solutions (e.g., Prometheus, ELK Stack).

- **Data Management:** Coordinating data between microservices can be complex. Implementing patterns like CQRS (Command Query Responsibility Segregation) and event sourcing can help.

- **Testing:** Comprehensive testing strategies, including unit tests, integration tests, and contract tests, are essential to ensure the reliability of microservices.

- **Deployment Strategies:** Implementing deployment strategies like blue-green deployments and canary releases minimizes the risk of deployment failures.

4. Best Practices for DevOps in Microservices:

- **Containerization:** Container technologies (e.g., Docker) facilitate packaging microservices and their dependencies for consistent deployment across environments.

- **Orchestration:** Orchestration platforms (e.g., Kubernetes) automate the deployment, scaling, and management of microservices in containerized environments.

- **Infrastructure as Code (IaC):** Use IaC tools to define and provision the infrastructure required to run microservices, ensuring consistency and reproducibility.

- **Security:** Implement security practices such as least privilege access, API security, and regular vulnerability scanning to protect microservices.

- **Culture and Collaboration:** Foster a DevOps culture of collaboration, shared responsibility, and continuous learning across development and operations teams.

5. Scalability and Growth:

- **Horizontal Scaling:** Microservices can be horizontally scaled to meet increasing demand, allowing organizations to optimize resource utilization.

- **Service Mesh:** Implementing a service mesh (e.g., Istio) can enhance communication, observability, and security in microservices architectures.

6. Challenges and Considerations:

- **Complexity:** Managing a large number of microservices can introduce operational complexity, requiring robust tooling and governance.

- **Data Consistency:** Maintaining data consistency and integrity across microservices can be challenging and requires careful design.

- **Distributed Systems Challenges:** Microservices introduce the complexities of distributed systems, including network latency, failures, and eventual consistency.

- **Cultural Shift:** Embracing a microservices architecture may necessitate a cultural shift within organizations, emphasizing autonomy, ownership, and collaboration.

In conclusion, DevOps practices are instrumental in realizing the potential of microservices architecture, allowing organizations to achieve agility, scalability, and rapid innovation. While implementing DevOps in microservices can be complex, organizations that invest in the right tools, practices, and cultural transformation will reap the rewards of a more flexible and responsive software development and deployment ecosystem.

B. DevOps for AI and Machine Learning: Bridging the Gap between Data and Deployment

The intersection of DevOps and AI/Machine Learning (ML) represents a dynamic frontier where software development and data science converge. This integration enables organizations to streamline the development, training, deployment, and management of AI/ML models, fostering innovation and agility. In this in-depth exploration, we'll delve into the complexities and opportunities of DevOps in AI/ML, including its core principles, benefits, challenges, and best practices.

1. Key Principles of DevOps in AI/ML:

- **Collaboration:** DevOps encourages cross-functional collaboration between data scientists, ML engineers, and operations teams, breaking down silos and ensuring a unified approach to model development and deployment.

- **Automation:** Automation is at the core of DevOps for AI/ML, encompassing tasks like data preprocessing, model training, testing, and deployment, with the goal of reducing manual interventions and achieving consistent results.

- **Continuous Integration/Continuous Deployment (CI/CD):** CI/CD pipelines are extended to include AI/ML workflows, enabling the automated testing, validation, and deployment of models into production.

- **Monitoring and Feedback:** Continuous monitoring of AI/ML models in production provides valuable feedback for model retraining and performance optimization, aligning with the DevOps principle of continuous improvement.

2. Benefits of DevOps in AI/ML:

- **Faster Model Deployment:** DevOps practices accelerate the deployment of AI/ML models from research to production, reducing time-to-market and enabling rapid experimentation.

- **Consistency and Reproducibility:** Automation ensures that model training and deployment processes are consistent and reproducible, minimizing variations that can affect model performance.

- **Scalability:** DevOps enables the scaling of AI/ML workloads to handle increased data volumes and model complexity, ensuring optimal resource utilization.

- **Model Monitoring and Governance:** DevOps practices facilitate the implementation of model monitoring, versioning, and governance, ensuring models are accountable, explainable, and compliant.

- **Collaboration:** Cross-functional collaboration between data scientists and operations teams fosters knowledge sharing and enables models to be production-ready.

3. Implementation Challenges and Solutions:

- **Data Management:** Managing and versioning datasets can be challenging. Implement data version control systems and data pipelines to ensure data consistency and reproducibility.

- **Experiment Tracking:** Tracking experiments and model versions is essential. Tools like MLflow and Kubeflow provide frameworks for tracking and managing experiments and model deployments.

- **Infrastructure Scaling:** Scalability of AI/ML workloads requires automated provisioning and orchestration using tools like Kubernetes and cloud-based solutions.

- **Model Monitoring:** Implement monitoring solutions to continuously assess model performance and detect deviations or drift.

- **Security:** Ensure that AI/ML models and data are secure through encryption, access controls, and regular security assessments.

4. Best Practices for DevOps in AI/ML:

- **Version Control:** Apply version control to both code and data to track changes and ensure reproducibility.

- **Continuous Integration:** Integrate model development workflows into CI pipelines, automating testing and validation.

- **Containerization:** Containerize AI/ML models and their dependencies for consistent deployment across environments.

- **Orchestration:** Use orchestration platforms to manage the deployment and scaling of AI/ML workloads.

- **Model Governance:** Implement governance policies and practices to ensure model compliance and accountability.

- **Collaborative Culture:** Foster a culture of collaboration and knowledge sharing between data scientists, ML engineers, and operations teams.

5. Scalability and Growth:

- **Model Deployment Strategies:** Implement deployment strategies that support model scaling, such as A/B testing and canary releases.

- **AutoML:** Explore automated machine learning (AutoML) solutions to streamline the model development process.

- **Edge Computing:** Consider deploying models at the edge to support real-time inference and reduce latency.

6. Challenges and Considerations:

- **Data Quality:** Ensuring data quality and consistency is crucial for building reliable AI/ML models.

- **Ethical and Bias Concerns:** Address ethical considerations and potential biases in AI/ML models to maintain fairness and transparency.

- **Resource Requirements:** AI/ML workloads can be resource-intensive, and managing infrastructure costs and scaling efficiently is essential.

- **Regulatory Compliance:** Ensure AI/ML models comply with data protection and regulatory requirements, especially in highly regulated industries.

In conclusion, DevOps for AI/ML bridges the gap between data science and deployment, enabling organizations to harness the power of AI/ML to drive innovation and competitiveness. By implementing DevOps principles, automation, and collaboration, organizations can accelerate their AI/ML initiatives while ensuring model reliability, scalability, and compliance with industry standards and ethical considerations.

C. Chaos Engineering: Forging Resilience through Controlled Disruption

Chaos Engineering is a discipline that has gained prominence in recent years as organizations seek to build more robust, resilient, and fault-tolerant software systems. It's a proactive approach to identifying and mitigating system weaknesses and vulnerabilities before they lead to costly outages or failures. In this in-depth exploration, we'll dive into the world of Chaos Engineering, examining its principles, methodologies, benefits, and best practices for building more resilient systems.

1. Principles of Chaos Engineering:

- **Proactive Approach:** Chaos Engineering is rooted in the philosophy that it's better to discover system weaknesses in a controlled and planned manner than to wait for them to manifest in unexpected and chaotic ways during real incidents.

- **Hypothesis-Driven:** Chaos Engineering is hypothesis-driven, meaning that engineers formulate hypotheses about how a system might fail and then conduct experiments to validate or refute those hypotheses.

- **Automation:** Chaos experiments are often automated to ensure repeatability and reduce the potential for human error. Automation tools orchestrate the introduction of controlled chaos into the system.

- **Observability:** Robust monitoring and observability are essential for Chaos Engineering. Engineers need to closely monitor system behavior during experiments to detect any anomalies.

- **Learning and Iteration:** Chaos Engineering is a continuous process of learning and iteration. Insights gained from experiments are used to improve system resilience over time.

2. Benefits of Chaos Engineering:

- **Resilience Testing:** Chaos Engineering allows organizations to stress-test their systems in a controlled environment, uncovering weaknesses and vulnerabilities before they impact users.

- **Fault Tolerance:** By intentionally injecting faults,

organizations can identify how their systems respond to failures and improve their fault tolerance mechanisms.

- **Reduced Downtime:** The proactive nature of Chaos Engineering helps organizations reduce downtime by addressing issues before they escalate into major incidents.

- **Cost Savings:** By preventing outages and minimizing downtime, organizations can achieve cost savings and maintain their reputation with customers.

- **Cultural Shift:** Chaos Engineering promotes a culture of accountability and resilience within organizations, encouraging teams to take ownership of system reliability.

3. Methodologies and Experimentation:

- **Hypothesis Formulation:** Engineers formulate hypotheses about how a system might fail or perform under certain conditions. For example, "What happens if we introduce high network latency?"

- **Experiment Design:** Chaos experiments are designed to test specific hypotheses. They include defining the scope of the experiment, selecting the target system or component, and specifying the failure injection.

- **Failure Injection:** Controlled chaos is introduced into the system by injecting failures, such as network delays, packet loss, resource exhaustion, or service unavailability.

- **Monitoring and Observability:** Comprehensive monitoring and observability tools are used to track system behavior during experiments and detect any anomalies or issues.

- **Automated Testing:** Many Chaos Engineering tools automate the process of injecting failures and monitoring system responses, ensuring repeatability and consistency.

4. Best Practices for Chaos Engineering:

- **Start Small:** Begin with small, well-defined experiments and gradually increase complexity as your organization gains experience with Chaos Engineering.

- **Safety First:** Implement safety measures to minimize the potential impact of chaos experiments on users. Always have a rollback plan.

- **Documentation:** Document your experiments, including the hypotheses, experiment design, and results. This helps teams learn from past experiments.

- **Cross-Functional Teams:** Involve cross-functional teams, including developers, operations, and QA, in Chaos Engineering efforts to gain diverse perspectives.

- **Feedback Loops:** Use insights from experiments to drive improvements in system architecture, fault tolerance mechanisms, and incident response processes.

5. Challenges and Considerations:

- **Complex Systems:** Chaos Engineering can be challenging in highly complex systems with many dependencies. Identifying the right experiments and understanding the potential impact is crucial.

- **Ethical Considerations:** Injecting chaos into a system can have ethical implications, especially in systems that handle sensitive data. Consider ethical guidelines and privacy regulations.

- **Resource Intensive:** Chaos experiments can be resource-intensive, both in terms of computing resources and personnel time. Plan accordingly.

- **Cultural Adoption:** Adopting Chaos Engineering may require a cultural shift within organizations to prioritize resilience and proactive failure testing.

In conclusion, Chaos Engineering is a valuable practice for organizations striving to build resilient and fault-tolerant systems in today's complex technology landscape. By intentionally injecting controlled chaos into their systems, organizations can uncover vulnerabilities, improve fault tolerance, reduce downtime, and foster a culture of resilience. While Chaos Engineering may pose challenges, the benefits of greater system reliability and improved user experience make it a worthwhile investment for modern organizations.

D. DevOps for Mobile and IoT: Accelerating Innovation in a Connected World

DevOps practices have transformed the software development and delivery landscape, and this transformation extends to the realms of mobile and Internet of Things (IoT) development. Mobile apps and IoT devices have become ubiquitous in our daily lives, and the demand for rapid development, continuous delivery, and robust maintenance is higher than ever. In this in-depth exploration, we'll delve into the intricacies of applying DevOps principles to mobile and IoT development, exploring its core principles, benefits, challenges, and best practices.

1. Key Principles of DevOps for Mobile and IoT:

- **Automation:** Automation is fundamental in DevOps for mobile and IoT. It encompasses building, testing, deployment, and monitoring processes to ensure consistency and efficiency.

- **Continuous Integration/Continuous Deployment (CI/CD):** CI/CD pipelines enable seamless integration of code changes, automated testing, and deployment to deliver updates rapidly.

- **Collaboration:** DevOps fosters collaboration among cross-functional teams, including developers, testers, operations, and product managers, ensuring a unified approach to development and operations.

- **Feedback Loops:** Continuous feedback from users and monitoring of mobile apps and IoT devices in the field inform development and maintenance efforts.

- **Security:** Security is a core consideration, with practices like code scanning, penetration testing, and secure update mechanisms being essential.

2. Benefits of DevOps for Mobile and IoT:

- **Rapid Delivery:** DevOps practices enable mobile apps and IoT devices to be developed and updated faster, addressing user needs and market demands more swiftly.

- **Stability and Reliability:** Continuous testing, monitoring, and automated rollback mechanisms ensure the stability and reliability of mobile and IoT applications, reducing downtime and enhancing user experience.

- **Security:** DevOps integrates security into every phase of development, making mobile apps and IoT devices more resilient against security threats.

- **Efficiency:** Automation streamlines development and deployment processes, reducing manual interventions and minimizing errors.

- **Scalability:** Mobile and IoT systems can easily scale to handle growing user bases and device ecosystems.

3. Implementation Challenges and Solutions:

- **Device Diversity:** In IoT, devices vary greatly in terms of hardware, software, and connectivity. Implement abstraction layers and device management solutions to handle this diversity.

- **Connectivity:** IoT devices may operate in challenging environments with intermittent connectivity. Implement offline capabilities and robust data synchronization mechanisms.

- **Security:** Mobile and IoT systems require robust security measures, including encryption, secure communication protocols, and regular security assessments.

- **Testing:** Testing mobile apps and IoT devices across different platforms and devices can be complex. Implement device farms, emulators, and simulators for comprehensive testing.

- **Data Management:** IoT devices generate vast amounts of data. Implement data storage, processing, and analytics solutions to handle this data effectively.

4. Best Practices for DevOps in Mobile and IoT:

- **Automated Testing:** Implement automated testing for mobile apps and IoT devices, covering unit tests, integration tests, and end-to-end tests.

- **CI/CD Pipelines:** Establish CI/CD pipelines for mobile apps and IoT firmware, enabling automated builds, tests, and deployments.

- **Monitoring and Telemetry:** Implement monitoring and telemetry solutions to collect data on device performance and user behavior.

- **Over-the-Air (OTA) Updates:** Develop robust OTA update mechanisms for IoT devices, allowing seamless and secure firmware updates.

- **Version Control:** Use version control systems for code and configuration management to track changes and maintain consistency.

5. Scalability and Growth:

- **Cloud Services:** Leverage cloud services to handle scalability and data processing requirements for IoT devices and mobile apps.

- **Edge Computing:** Consider edge computing solutions to process data closer to the source, reducing latency and enhancing real-time capabilities.

- **Containerization:** Containerization of mobile app components and microservices can simplify deployment and scaling.

6. Challenges and Considerations:

- **Device Lifecycle Management:** Managing the lifecycle of IoT devices, including provisioning, maintenance, and decommissioning, can be complex and resource-intensive.

- **Regulatory Compliance:** Mobile and IoT applications may need to adhere to specific regulations and compliance standards, requiring careful consideration during development.

- **Privacy Concerns:** IoT devices often collect sensitive data. Ensure robust data protection and privacy mechanisms to address user concerns.

- **Scalability Planning:** Planning for the scalability of mobile and IoT systems is critical to handle growing user bases and device fleets.

In conclusion, applying DevOps practices to mobile and IoT development empowers organizations to build, deploy, and maintain robust and innovative solutions in a rapidly evolving technological landscape. By embracing automation, collaboration, and continuous improvement, organizations can meet user demands, ensure system reliability, enhance security, and drive innovation in the mobile and IoT domains.

E. DevOps for Legacy Systems: Modernizing the Past for the Future

Legacy systems are the backbone of many organizations, providing critical functionality but often burdened by outdated technology, complexity, and maintenance challenges. DevOps, with its emphasis on automation, collaboration, and continuous improvement, can breathe new life into these systems, making them more agile, reliable, and cost-effective. In this in-depth exploration, we'll delve into the complexities of applying DevOps principles to legacy systems, examining its core principles, benefits, challenges, and best practices.

1. Key Principles of DevOps for Legacy Systems:

- **Automation:** Automation is a cornerstone of DevOps, and it's equally crucial for legacy systems. Automating repetitive tasks, such as deployment, testing, and configuration management, reduces human error and accelerates processes.

- **Collaboration:** Cross-functional collaboration is essential, bringing together developers, operations teams, and other stakeholders to work collectively on legacy system modernization.

- **Incremental Changes:** Legacy systems often resist radical overhauls. DevOps emphasizes incremental changes, allowing organizations to gradually modernize and improve existing systems.

- **Continuous Improvement:** DevOps encourages organizations to continuously evaluate and enhance their processes, which is particularly important when dealing with legacy systems that require ongoing maintenance and updates.

- **Monitoring and Feedback:** Robust monitoring and feedback mechanisms help identify and address issues in legacy systems, leading to more reliable performance.

2. Benefits of DevOps for Legacy Systems:

- **Increased Agility:** DevOps practices enable organizations to make changes to legacy systems more quickly and respond to evolving business needs.

- **Reduced Downtime:** Automation and improved testing practices reduce the risk of downtime during updates and maintenance activities.

- **Cost Savings:** By automating manual processes and

improving efficiency, DevOps can reduce the operational costs associated with legacy systems.

- **Enhanced Reliability:** Continuous monitoring and feedback loops help identify and address reliability issues in legacy systems.

- **Risk Mitigation:** Incremental changes and automated testing reduce the risk of introducing new problems while modernizing legacy systems.

3. Implementation Challenges and Solutions:

- **Legacy Codebase:** Working with legacy code can be challenging due to its age, complexity, and lack of documentation. Implement strategies like code refactoring, modularization, and code analysis tools to improve code quality.

- **Lack of Automation:** Legacy systems often lack automation, making it difficult to implement DevOps practices. Begin by automating low-risk, repetitive tasks, and gradually expand automation efforts.

- **Resistance to Change:** Teams and stakeholders may be resistant to change, especially when dealing with mission-critical legacy systems. Implement change management strategies and demonstrate the benefits of modernization.

- **Limited Testing:** Legacy systems may not have comprehensive test suites. Invest in testing infrastructure and create automated tests to ensure that changes do not introduce regressions.

- **Data Migration:** If modernizing a legacy system involves migrating data, plan for this carefully and ensure data integrity during the process.

4. Best Practices for DevOps in Legacy Systems:

- **Start Small:** Begin with small, well-defined projects or areas within the legacy system for modernization, gradually expanding as confidence and experience grow.

- **Automated Testing:** Implement automated testing to ensure that changes do not introduce new issues. Create test cases that cover critical functionality.

- **Version Control:** Implement version control for the legacy codebase to track changes and facilitate collaboration among teams.

- **Continuous Integration/Continuous Deployment:** Establish CI/CD pipelines for the legacy system to automate testing and deployment processes.

- **Documentation:** Improve documentation for the legacy system to enhance understanding and facilitate knowledge transfer.

5. Scalability and Growth:

- **Microservices:** Consider breaking down monolithic legacy systems into microservices, making them more modular and easier to maintain.

- **Cloud Migration:** Migrating legacy systems to cloud infrastructure can provide scalability and cost benefits.

- **Containerization:** Containerizing legacy applications can simplify deployment and improve scalability.

6. Challenges and Considerations:

- **Risk Management:** Modernizing legacy systems carries risks, including potential disruption of critical business processes. Develop risk mitigation strategies and contingency plans.

- **Regulatory Compliance:** Legacy systems in regulated industries must adhere to compliance standards. Ensure that modernization efforts maintain compliance.

- **Budget and Resources:** Modernizing legacy systems requires budget and resources. Secure support and funding from stakeholders.

- **Cultural Shift:** Implementing DevOps practices in a legacy system environment may require a cultural shift. Encourage a culture of collaboration, experimentation, and continuous improvement.

In conclusion, applying DevOps practices to legacy systems offers a path to modernization, increased agility, and improved reliability. While the challenges are significant, organizations that invest in modernizing their legacy systems can unlock value, reduce operational costs, and better position themselves for the evolving needs of the business. DevOps is a key enabler of this transformation, guiding organizations toward a more flexible and responsive approach to legacy system management.

CHAPTER 11

DevOps Culture and Transformation

DevOps isn't just about tools and practices; it's a cultural transformation that redefines how organizations approach software development, delivery, and operations. In this introductory exploration, we embark on a journey into the heart of DevOps culture and transformation. We'll explore the principles, values, and practices that underpin DevOps and how organizations can embark on this transformative journey to foster collaboration, innovation, and agility across their teams and processes.

A. Cultural Transformation Strategies in DevOps: Fostering Collaboration and Innovation

Cultural transformation lies at the core of DevOps, reshaping the way organizations approach technology, collaboration, and continuous improvement. To succeed in implementing DevOps practices effectively, organizations must adopt strategies that nurture a culture conducive to DevOps principles. In this in-depth exploration, we'll delve into the strategies and principles for cultural transformation in DevOps.

1. Leadership Buy-In and Support:

- **Setting the Example:** Transformation starts at the top. Leaders must actively endorse and exemplify DevOps principles, demonstrating their commitment to change.

- **Empowering Teams:** Leaders should empower teams to make decisions and take ownership of their work. Trusting teams to drive change fosters a culture of responsibility and accountability.

- **Removing Barriers:** Leaders should identify and remove organizational barriers that hinder collaboration and efficiency, whether they are bureaucratic, technical, or cultural.

2. Communication and Transparency:

- **Open Communication:** Encourage open and honest communication across teams and departments. This includes sharing successes, failures, and challenges openly.

- **Cross-Functional Collaboration:** Promote collaboration between traditionally siloed teams, such as development, operations, and quality assurance. Cross-functional teams work together to solve problems and achieve shared goals.

- **Shared Metrics:** Define and share key performance indicators (KPIs) that are aligned with DevOps goals. Transparency in performance metrics helps teams measure progress and identify areas for improvement.

3. Education and Training:

- **Continuous Learning:** Invest in continuous learning and skill development for employees. Provide access to training and resources that support DevOps practices and technologies.

- **Certifications:** Encourage team members to pursue relevant certifications, such as those for cloud platforms, automation tools, and DevOps methodologies.

- **Mentorship and Knowledge Sharing:** Establish mentorship programs and encourage knowledge sharing within the organization. Learning from peers and experienced practitioners accelerates skill development.

4. Collaboration and Cross-Functional Teams:

- **Cross-Functional Teams:** Form cross-functional teams that bring together members from various disciplines, such as development, operations, security, and quality assurance, to work on projects collaboratively.

- **Shared Responsibility:** Foster a sense of shared responsibility for the entire software development lifecycle, from coding and testing to deployment and maintenance.

- **Blame-Free Culture:** Promote a culture where individuals are not blamed for failures but encouraged to learn from them and prevent recurrence.

5. Automation and Tooling:

- **Automation-First Mindset:** Encourage teams to automate repetitive tasks and processes wherever possible. Automation frees up time for more strategic and creative work.

- **Tooling Selection:** Invest in the right tools that support DevOps practices, such as CI/CD pipelines, infrastructure as code (IaC), and monitoring solutions.

- **Tool Training:** Provide training and support for the tools and technologies that teams use. Proficiency with DevOps tools is essential for efficiency.

6. Feedback Loops:

- **Continuous Feedback:** Implement feedback mechanisms at every stage of the development process. This includes feedback from users, testing, monitoring, and incident response.

- **Incident Reviews:** Conduct post-incident reviews (post-mortems) to analyze what went wrong, why, and how to prevent similar incidents in the future. Focus on learning, not blame.

- **User Feedback:** Collect and incorporate feedback from end-users to guide product improvements and enhancements.

7. Cultural Change Metrics:

- **Measure Progress:** Define and track cultural transformation metrics. These could include collaboration scores, deployment frequency, mean time to resolution (MTTR), and employee engagement surveys.

- **Regular Assessments:** Periodically assess the cultural transformation journey to identify areas that need improvement and to celebrate successes.

8. Continuous Improvement:

- **Kaizen Philosophy:** Embrace the Kaizen philosophy of continuous improvement. Encourage teams to regularly reflect on their processes and seek opportunities for refinement.

- **Experimentation:** Encourage experimentation and innovation. Create a culture where it's safe to try new approaches, even if they may lead to failures, as long as learning is the outcome.

9. Scaling DevOps Culture:

- **Scaling Strategies:** Develop strategies for scaling DevOps culture across the organization, especially in larger enterprises. This may involve replicating successful cultural changes in different departments or regions.

- **Champion Networks:** Identify and empower DevOps champions within the organization who can advocate for and support cultural transformation.

In conclusion, cultural transformation in DevOps is a journey that requires commitment, patience, and ongoing effort. By embracing leadership support, transparent communication, continuous learning, collaboration, and automation, organizations can create a culture that promotes agility, innovation, and resilience, ultimately leading to successful DevOps adoption and improved business outcomes.

B. Leadership in DevOps: Nurturing a Culture of Innovation and Collaboration

Effective leadership is essential for the successful implementation of DevOps practices within an organization. In DevOps, leaders play a crucial role in driving cultural transformation, fostering collaboration, and aligning teams towards shared goals. In this in-depth exploration, we'll delve into the key aspects of leadership in DevOps, highlighting the principles, responsibilities, and strategies that contribute to a culture of innovation and collaboration.

1. Leading by Example:

- **Embracing DevOps Principles:** DevOps leaders must lead by example by fully embracing the principles of DevOps themselves. This includes demonstrating a commitment to automation, collaboration, continuous improvement, and shared responsibility.

- **Adopting a Growth Mindset:** Leaders should encourage a growth mindset within their teams, emphasizing that failure is an opportunity for learning and improvement rather than a cause for blame.

- **Continuous Learning:** DevOps is a rapidly evolving field. Leaders should demonstrate a commitment to continuous learning, staying up-to-date with the latest tools, practices, and industry trends.

2. Empowering Teams:

- **Autonomous Teams:** DevOps leaders should empower teams to make decisions and take ownership of their work. Autonomous teams are more motivated and agile in responding to challenges.

- **Removing Barriers:** Leaders should identify and address organizational barriers that hinder collaboration and efficiency. This includes breaking down silos between traditionally separate teams, such as development and operations.

- **Trust Building:** Trust is essential for collaboration. Leaders build trust by being transparent, reliable, and supportive of their teams.

3. Communication and Collaboration:

- **Open and Transparent Communication:** DevOps leaders should encourage open and honest communication across teams and departments. Transparency in decision-making processes fosters trust and alignment.

- **Cross-Functional Collaboration:** Promote collaboration between traditionally siloed teams, such as development, operations, quality assurance, security, and business stakeholders. Cross-functional teams work together to solve problems and achieve shared goals.

- **Alignment with Business Goals:** Ensure that DevOps initiatives are aligned with broader business objectives. Leaders should be able to articulate how DevOps practices contribute to the organization's success.

4. Setting Clear Goals and Expectations:

- **Defining DevOps Goals:** Leaders should define clear goals and expectations for DevOps adoption within the organization. These goals should be specific, measurable, achievable, relevant, and time-bound (SMART).

- **Performance Metrics:** Establish performance metrics and key performance indicators (KPIs) that align with DevOps goals. Metrics help track progress and identify areas for improvement.

- **Regular Reviews:** Conduct regular reviews to assess progress toward DevOps goals. Adjust strategies and approaches as needed to stay on course.

5. Building a Learning Culture:

- **Continuous Learning:** Encourage a culture of continuous learning and improvement. Leaders should support team members in acquiring new skills and knowledge relevant to DevOps practices.

- **Mentoring and Coaching:** DevOps leaders can provide mentoring and coaching to team members, helping them develop their skills and navigate challenges effectively.

- **Learning from Failures:** Foster a culture where failures are viewed as opportunities for learning and improvement rather than reasons for blame. Encourage teams to conduct post-incident reviews and share lessons learned.

6. Leading Change:

- **Change Management:** Effective leaders understand that cultural transformation is a journey. They should implement change management strategies that help employees adapt to new practices and mindsets.

- **Resistance Management:** Not all team members may immediately embrace DevOps practices. Leaders should actively address resistance to change, seeking to understand concerns and provide guidance.

- **Celebrating Successes:** Celebrate successes and milestones along the DevOps journey. Recognizing and rewarding achievements helps maintain motivation and enthusiasm.

7. Diversity and Inclusion:

- **Inclusive Leadership:** Inclusive leaders value diversity and actively seek different perspectives and ideas. Diversity in teams fosters innovation and creativity.

- **Equity:** Leaders should ensure that opportunities and resources are distributed equitably among team members, regardless of background or identity.

8. Scaling Leadership:

- **Champion Networks:** Identify and empower DevOps

champions within the organization who can advocate for DevOps principles, provide support to teams, and drive cultural transformation.

- **Leadership at All Levels:** DevOps leadership is not limited to upper management. Encourage leadership behaviors at all levels of the organization, as each individual can contribute to the culture of innovation and collaboration.

In conclusion, leadership is a pivotal factor in the successful adoption of DevOps practices. DevOps leaders should embody the principles of DevOps, empower teams, facilitate communication and collaboration, and drive a culture of continuous learning and improvement. By doing so, they can lead their organizations towards greater agility, innovation, and competitiveness in today's fast-paced technology landscape.

C. Overcoming Resistance to Change in DevOps: Navigating the Path to Transformation

Resistance to change is a common challenge organizations face when implementing DevOps practices and cultural transformation. People are naturally inclined to maintain the status quo, especially when it comes to changes that can disrupt established workflows and routines. In this in-depth exploration, we'll delve into the reasons behind resistance to change and strategies to overcome it within the context of DevOps adoption.

1. Understanding Resistance to Change:

- **Fear of the Unknown:** Change often brings uncertainty. Team members may fear that DevOps practices will disrupt their roles or that they lack the necessary skills to adapt.

- **Loss of Control:** People value a sense of control over their work. DevOps can involve relinquishing some control in favor of automation and collaboration, which can be unsettling.

- **Comfort with the Status Quo:** People become accustomed to their existing workflows and processes, even if they are inefficient. Change requires stepping out of one's comfort zone.

- **Lack of Awareness:** Some team members may not fully understand the benefits of DevOps or the rationale behind the changes, leading to skepticism.

2. Strategies for Overcoming Resistance:

- **1. Leadership Buy-In and Support:**

Engage leadership early in the change process. When leaders visibly support and endorse DevOps practices, it sends a clear message that the change is a strategic priority.

- **2. Communication and Education:**

Open and transparent communication is vital. Explain the reasons for adopting DevOps, the benefits it will bring to the organization, and the vision for the future. Provide education and training opportunities to bridge knowledge gaps.

- **3. Involvement and Collaboration:**

Involve team members in the decision-making process. Collaborate on defining DevOps practices and processes, allowing team members to have a say in how changes are implemented.

- **4. Pilot Projects:**

Start with small, low-risk pilot projects to demonstrate the benefits of DevOps in a tangible way. Success stories from pilot projects can inspire confidence in the change.

- **5. Continuous Feedback and Improvement:**

Create feedback loops that allow team members to express concerns, ask questions, and provide input. Use feedback to make iterative improvements to the DevOps implementation.

- **6. Change Agents and Champions:**

Identify change agents and champions within the organization—individuals who are enthusiastic about DevOps and can help influence and support their peers.

- **7. Celebrate Successes:**

Celebrate milestones and successes along the DevOps journey. Recognizing and rewarding achievements can boost morale and motivation.

- **8. Clear Roles and Expectations:**

Define clear roles and expectations for team members within the context of DevOps. Knowing their new responsibilities and contributions can reduce uncertainty.

- **9. Addressing Fear and Anxiety:**

Provide reassurance that changes will be gradual, and team members will receive the necessary training and support to adapt. Address specific fears and concerns openly.

- **10. Persistence and Patience:**

Change takes time, and resistance may persist. DevOps leaders should remain persistent, patient, and empathetic throughout the transformation process.

3. Dealing with Specific Types of Resistance:

- **Technical Resistance:** Address technical resistance by providing training and resources to help team members acquire the necessary skills and competencies for DevOps practices.

- **Cultural Resistance:** Cultural resistance may stem from ingrained beliefs and values within the organization. Leaders should actively promote the desired DevOps culture and address cultural barriers.

- **Political Resistance:** Address political resistance by involving key stakeholders in decision-making and ensuring that changes align with the organization's strategic goals.

- **Individual Resistance:** Some individuals may resist change due to personal preferences or fears. Work with these individuals on a one-on-one basis to understand their concerns and provide support.

4. Monitoring Progress:

- Establish metrics and key performance indicators (KPIs) to measure the progress of DevOps adoption and cultural transformation. Regularly review these metrics to assess the effectiveness of change strategies.

5. Adapting to Feedback:

- Be willing to adapt and refine change strategies based on feedback and the evolving needs of the organization. Change is an ongoing process.

In conclusion, overcoming resistance to change is a critical aspect of successful DevOps adoption. By understanding the sources of resistance, engaging leadership support, fostering open communication, and using targeted strategies, organizations can navigate the path to transformation more effectively. A DevOps culture that embraces change, continuous improvement, and collaboration is within reach for organizations that are willing to invest in overcoming resistance and fostering a culture of innovation and agility.

D. Scaling DevOps in Large Organizations: Navigating Complexity for Agile Transformation

DevOps practices have proven their worth in improving collaboration, increasing speed to market, and enhancing software quality. However, implementing DevOps at scale in large organizations presents unique challenges due to the complexity of operations, multiple teams, legacy systems, and diverse stakeholders. In this in-depth exploration, we'll delve into strategies and considerations for successfully scaling DevOps in large and complex enterprises.

1. DevOps Principles for Large-Scale Adoption:

- **1.1. Automation:**

Automation remains a core tenet of DevOps at scale. It encompasses not only the automation of repetitive tasks but also the automation of compliance, testing, and deployment pipelines. Implementing robust automation helps reduce manual intervention and ensures consistency across a large organization.

- **1.2. Collaboration:**

Collaboration across teams is essential. Large organizations often consist of various siloed departments, and DevOps aims to break down these silos. Cross-functional teams, shared goals, and open communication channels are key to fostering collaboration.

- **1.3. Continuous Improvement:**

Embrace a culture of continuous improvement at all levels. Encourage teams to regularly reflect on their processes, seek feedback, and implement iterative changes. Large organizations should view DevOps as an ongoing journey rather than a destination.

- **1.4. Feedback Loops:**

Establish feedback loops throughout the software development lifecycle. This includes feedback from users, automated testing, monitoring, and incident response. Rapid feedback helps teams identify and address issues promptly.

- **1.5. Small Batches:**

Promote the practice of breaking down work into small,

manageable batches. This reduces the complexity of changes and allows for more frequent releases, improving agility.

2. Organizational Structure:

- ### 2.1. DevOps Teams vs. Distributed Ownership:

Large organizations often debate whether to create dedicated DevOps teams or distribute DevOps responsibilities among existing teams. The choice depends on the organization's culture and goals. Dedicated teams can focus on tooling, best practices, and culture, while distributed ownership encourages accountability within individual teams.

- ### 2.2. Center of Excellence (CoE):

Establish a DevOps Center of Excellence to provide guidance, best practices, and support for DevOps adoption. The CoE can facilitate knowledge sharing and standardization across the organization.

- ### 2.3. Scaling Agile Frameworks:

Many large organizations adopt agile frameworks like SAFe (Scaled Agile Framework) or LeSS (Large-Scale Scrum) to align DevOps practices with agile methodologies at scale. These frameworks provide structure and guidance for large-scale agility.

3. Technology and Tools:

- ### 3.1. Standardization:

Standardize on a set of DevOps tools and technologies. Having a consistent toolchain simplifies management and reduces complexity. However, allow flexibility for teams to choose the specific tools that best suit their needs.

- ### 3.2. Cloud and Containerization:

Leveraging cloud services and containerization (e.g., Docker and Kubernetes) can enhance scalability and resource management, enabling teams to build, test, and deploy applications more efficiently.

- ### 3.3. DevOps as Code:

Implement infrastructure as code (IaC) and treat DevOps practices themselves as code. This enables version control, automation, and reproducibility of DevOps processes.

- ### 3.4. Monitoring and Observability:

Invest in robust monitoring and observability solutions. Large organizations typically manage a multitude of services, and real-time insights into system performance are essential for quick issue resolution.

4. Culture and Communication:

- ### 4.1. Leadership Buy-In:

Secure buy-in from senior leadership, as their support is crucial for cultural change and resource allocation. Leaders should model the desired DevOps culture and practices.

- ### 4.2. Communication Channels:

Establish clear communication channels for disseminating information and fostering collaboration. This includes regular meetings, reporting structures, and shared documentation.

- ### 4.3. Communities of Practice:

Encourage the formation of DevOps communities of practice (CoPs). These self-organized groups allow practitioners to share knowledge, experiences, and best practices across the organization.

- ### 4.4. Change Management:

Recognize that cultural transformation is a gradual process. Implement change management strategies to address resistance and ensure alignment with DevOps values.

5. Metrics and Key Performance Indicators (KPIs):

- Define and track relevant metrics and KPIs at both the team and organizational levels. Metrics may include deployment frequency, lead time, change failure rate, and customer satisfaction. Regularly review and adapt these metrics to drive continuous improvement.

6. Security and Compliance:

- ### 6.1. DevSecOps:

Integrate security practices into DevOps processes from the outset. DevSecOps emphasizes security as a shared responsibility and incorporates security checks and compliance as code.

- ### 6.2. Compliance as Code:

Implement compliance as code to automate and enforce regulatory requirements and internal policies consistently.

7. Scaling Challenges and Solutions:

- ### 7.1. Legacy Systems:

Legacy systems can pose challenges for DevOps adoption. Gradual modernization, containerization, and infrastructure as code can help integrate legacy systems into the DevOps pipeline.

- ### 7.2. Cultural Resistance:

Address cultural resistance by actively promoting DevOps values, fostering a culture of experimentation and learning, and providing continuous education.

- ### 7.3. Coordination and Dependency Management:

Large organizations often have complex dependencies between teams and systems. Effective coordination and dependency management are critical to avoid bottlenecks and delays.

8. Governance and Risk Management:

- Implement governance frameworks that balance the need for innovation with risk management. Define policies, guidelines, and guardrails to ensure compliance while enabling agility.

In conclusion, scaling DevOps in large organizations is a complex but rewarding endeavor. It requires a holistic approach that combines cultural transformation, technology adoption, organizational structure, and effective communication. By embracing DevOps principles and tailoring strategies to the organization's unique challenges, large enterprises can achieve greater agility, innovation, and competitiveness in today's fast-paced digital landscape.

CHAPTER 12

Case Studies and Success Stories

In the realm of DevOps, real-world experiences and success stories serve as beacons of inspiration and guidance for organizations seeking to embark on their own transformative journeys. In this section, we delve into case studies and success stories that showcase how various industries and enterprises have harnessed the power of DevOps to overcome challenges, drive innovation, and achieve remarkable outcomes. These stories illuminate the path forward, offering valuable insights, strategies, and practical lessons learned from those who have successfully navigated the DevOps landscape.

A. Real-World DevOps Implementations: Unpacking Success Stories

DevOps is not just a theoretical concept; it's a set of practices and principles that have been applied with remarkable success in real-world scenarios across diverse industries. These real-world DevOps implementations serve as tangible evidence of the transformative power of DevOps in improving software delivery, enhancing collaboration, and achieving business goals. In this in-depth exploration, we'll dive into several real-world DevOps success stories, highlighting the challenges, strategies, and outcomes that have made them noteworthy.

1. Netflix: Continuous Deployment and Resilience

- **Challenge:** Netflix, a leading streaming service, faced the challenge of deploying thousands of changes to its production environment each day while maintaining service reliability.

- **DevOps Solution:** Netflix embraced a culture of "Freedom and Responsibility" by empowering development teams to own their services end-to-end. They implemented a fully automated CI/CD pipeline that enabled continuous deployment and rollback capabilities.

- **Outcome:** Netflix achieved remarkable resilience and scalability. Their approach to DevOps allows them to handle sudden traffic spikes, optimize content delivery, and provide a seamless streaming experience for millions of users worldwide.

2. Amazon: Infrastructure as Code (IaC)

- **Challenge:** Amazon Web Services (AWS) needed to manage the vast and rapidly growing infrastructure required to support its cloud services.

- **DevOps Solution:** Amazon adopted Infrastructure as Code (IaC) principles, using tools like AWS CloudFormation. This allowed them to define and manage infrastructure resources through code, automating provisioning and scaling.

- **Outcome:** IaC improved resource management, reduced manual errors, and enabled rapid scaling. It became a foundational practice not only for AWS but also for many organizations using cloud services.

3. Etsy: Continuous Delivery and Culture

- **Challenge:** Etsy, an e-commerce platform, wanted to accelerate software delivery while maintaining product quality and fostering a culture of experimentation.

- **DevOps Solution:** Etsy embraced a culture of "Code as Craft" and implemented continuous delivery practices. They automated testing, deployments, and monitoring, enabling multiple releases per day.

- **Outcome:** Etsy achieved faster time-to-market and empowered its engineering teams to experiment and innovate. The culture of transparency and continuous improvement became a hallmark of their DevOps journey.

4. Target: DevOps for Legacy Systems

- **Challenge:** Target, a retail giant, needed to modernize and improve its legacy systems to compete in the digital age.

- **DevOps Solution:** Target adopted a "Test-Driven Development" (TDD) approach and implemented DevOps practices for legacy systems. They automated testing, infrastructure provisioning, and deployment processes.

- **Outcome:** Target improved system reliability, reduced downtime, and enhanced the customer experience. DevOps practices helped them make their legacy systems more agile and adaptable.

5. Capital One: Security and Compliance

- **Challenge:** Capital One, a financial institution, had to balance the need for speed in software development with stringent security and compliance requirements.

- **DevOps Solution:** Capital One embraced the concept of "DevSecOps" by integrating security into the DevOps pipeline. They automated security checks, implemented compliance as code, and monitored for vulnerabilities.

- **Outcome:** Capital One improved its security posture while maintaining agility. DevSecOps practices enabled faster threat detection and response, reducing security risks.

6. NASA: DevOps for Space Exploration

- **Challenge:** NASA faced the challenge of managing complex software systems for space exploration missions with high reliability requirements.

- **DevOps Solution:** NASA's Jet Propulsion Laboratory (JPL) adopted DevOps practices to improve software development and deployment for missions like the Mars rovers. They automated testing and deployment processes.

- **Outcome:** JPL achieved more efficient mission operations, reduced risks, and improved collaboration among teams. DevOps practices played a critical role in the success of missions like Curiosity and Perseverance.

These real-world DevOps implementations demonstrate that the principles and practices of DevOps are adaptable and beneficial across various domains. They illustrate the importance of cultural transformation, automation, continuous improvement, and collaboration in achieving remarkable outcomes. By drawing inspiration from these success stories, organizations can tailor DevOps practices to their specific needs and embark on their own journeys towards agility, innovation, and excellence.

B. Industry-Specific Use Cases: How DevOps Drives Innovation

DevOps practices are not one-size-fits-all; they can be tailored to meet the unique challenges and requirements of different industries. In this in-depth exploration, we'll delve into industry-specific use cases to understand how DevOps is driving innovation and transforming processes in various sectors.

1. Healthcare: Enhancing Patient Care and Compliance

- **Challenge:** Healthcare organizations are tasked with delivering high-quality patient care while complying with strict regulatory requirements, such as HIPAA in the United States.

- **DevOps Solution:** DevOps in healthcare involves automating software testing, deployment, and infrastructure provisioning. This enables faster development and deployment of electronic health records (EHR) systems, telemedicine applications, and patient portals while ensuring compliance.

- **Outcome:** DevOps in healthcare has led to improved patient care through more accessible and efficient health IT systems. It has also helped organizations maintain compliance by automating security and compliance checks.

2. Finance: Speeding Up Financial Services

- **Challenge:** The financial industry demands rapid innovation and customer service while managing complex, highly regulated systems.

- **DevOps Solution:** DevOps practices in finance enable faster development and deployment of trading platforms, mobile banking apps, and risk management systems. Automation is critical for ensuring security and compliance while delivering updates quickly.

- **Outcome:** DevOps has increased the speed of financial service delivery, reduced errors, and enhanced customer experience. Real-time trading, mobile banking, and AI-powered risk management are just a few examples of innovations driven by DevOps in finance.

3. Automotive: Accelerating Vehicle Development

- **Challenge:** The automotive industry faces intense competition and customer demands for innovative features in vehicles.

- **DevOps Solution:** DevOps in automotive streamlines software development and deployment for in-car infotainment systems, autonomous driving features, and vehicle connectivity. Continuous testing ensures safety and reliability.

- **Outcome:** DevOps has reduced time-to-market for new vehicle features and software updates. It has also facilitated remote diagnostics and over-the-air software updates for vehicles.

4. Retail: E-Commerce and Customer Experience

- **Challenge:** Retailers need to keep up with changing consumer preferences and deliver a seamless online shopping experience.

- **DevOps Solution:** DevOps practices in retail focus on e-commerce platforms, inventory management systems, and customer-facing apps. Automation helps manage peak traffic during sales events, and A/B testing improves user experience.

- **Outcome:** DevOps enables retailers to quickly adapt to market trends, scale their online presence during high-demand periods, and provide personalized shopping experiences.

5. Gaming: Continuous Delivery of Entertainment

- **Challenge:** The gaming industry must release new games, updates, and patches while maintaining game stability.

- **DevOps Solution:** DevOps in gaming automates game build processes, testing, and deployment. Continuous integration allows developers to quickly address bugs and release new content.

- **Outcome:** DevOps accelerates game development and provides players with timely updates and content. It also helps identify and fix in-game issues more efficiently.

6. Aerospace: Mission-Critical Systems

- **Challenge:** Aerospace companies must ensure the reliability and safety of mission-critical systems for space exploration and aviation.

- **DevOps Solution:** DevOps practices in aerospace involve automated testing and deployment for control systems, satellite software, and navigation systems. Rigorous testing is essential to ensure system reliability.

- **Outcome:** DevOps enhances the efficiency of aerospace system development, enabling faster launches and more reliable mission outcomes. Automated processes reduce human errors in complex systems.

7. Energy: Optimizing Infrastructure

- **Challenge:** Energy companies need to optimize their infrastructure for efficiency and sustainability while managing complex systems.

- **DevOps Solution:** DevOps in the energy sector involves automation of processes related to grid management, energy trading, and monitoring of renewable energy sources. It enables real-time decision-making and reduces downtime.

- **Outcome:** DevOps improves energy infrastructure management, enhances grid reliability, and supports the transition to cleaner energy sources.

These industry-specific use cases demonstrate that DevOps is a versatile approach that can be applied across various sectors to drive innovation, improve customer experiences, and ensure compliance and safety. By tailoring DevOps practices to their unique challenges and goals, organizations can harness the full potential of DevOps to stay competitive and meet the evolving needs of their industries.

C. Navigating Challenges and Finding Solutions in DevOps

While DevOps offers numerous benefits, its implementation is not without challenges. Understanding these challenges and developing effective solutions is essential for a successful DevOps journey. In this in-depth exploration, we'll delve into some common challenges faced by organizations when adopting DevOps practices and explore solutions to overcome them.

1. Cultural Resistance:

- **Challenge:** Resistance to cultural change is one of the primary obstacles in DevOps adoption. Teams accustomed to siloed operations may resist the idea of cross-functional collaboration and shared responsibilities.

- **Solution:**

    - **Leadership Buy-In:** Leadership support is crucial in driving cultural change. Leaders should model the desired DevOps behavior, endorse collaboration, and communicate the strategic importance of DevOps.

- **Education and Training:** Provide training and workshops to help team members understand the value of DevOps and acquire the necessary skills. Foster a culture of continuous learning and improvement.

- **Communities of Practice:** Establish communities of practice (CoPs) where team members can share experiences, challenges, and best practices. CoPs promote knowledge sharing and collaboration.

2. Lack of Automation:

- **Challenge:** Manual processes and lack of automation can lead to inefficiencies, errors, and slower development cycles.

- **Solution:**

  - **Automation-First Mindset:** Encourage an "automation-first" mindset where teams prioritize automating repetitive tasks and manual processes.

  - **DevOps Tools:** Invest in DevOps tools for continuous integration, continuous deployment, and infrastructure as code. These tools streamline automation efforts.

  - **Continuous Testing:** Implement automated testing at

every stage of the pipeline to catch issues early and reduce the manual testing burden.

3. Complexity in Legacy Systems:

- **Challenge:** Legacy systems often have outdated architectures and complex dependencies that make DevOps adoption challenging.

- **Solution:**

    - **Gradual Modernization:** Start by containerizing legacy applications to make them more portable and manageable. Implement microservices architectures to gradually modernize.

    - **Infrastructure as Code (IaC):** Use IaC to automate the provisioning and management of legacy system environments. This makes infrastructure more predictable and reproducible.

4. Security and Compliance:

- **Challenge:** Integrating security and compliance into DevOps pipelines is essential but can be challenging, especially in regulated industries.

- **Solution:**

    - **DevSecOps:** Adopt the DevSecOps approach by

integrating security practices into every stage of the development pipeline. Use automated security scans and compliance checks.

- **Compliance as Code:** Define compliance requirements as code, making it possible to automate compliance checks and demonstrate adherence to regulations.

5. Scalability and Resource Management:

- **Challenge:** As organizations grow, scaling DevOps practices and managing resources efficiently become increasingly complex.

- **Solution:**

  - **Cloud and Containers:** Leverage cloud services and containerization (e.g., Docker and Kubernetes) for scalable and resource-efficient infrastructure.

  - **Scalable CI/CD Pipelines:** Design CI/CD pipelines that can scale automatically to handle increased workloads during peak periods.

6. Communication and Collaboration:

- **Challenge:** Effective communication and collaboration between development, operations, and other stakeholders are crucial but can be hindered by silos.

- **Solution:**

  - **Cross-Functional Teams:** Encourage cross-functional teams that include developers, operations, and other relevant roles to promote collaboration.

  - **Collaboration Tools:** Use collaboration tools like chat platforms and project management software to facilitate communication and transparency.

  - **Feedback Loops:** Establish feedback loops for continuous improvement and to address issues promptly.

7. Monitoring and Observability:

- **Challenge:** Without proper monitoring and observability, identifying and resolving issues in real-time becomes difficult.

- **Solution:**

  - **Monitoring Tools:** Implement robust monitoring tools that provide visibility into application and infrastructure performance.

  - **Alerting and Automation:** Set up automated alerting based on predefined thresholds to detect and address issues proactively.

8. Resistance to Change:

- **Challenge:** Resistance to DevOps practices can come from individuals or teams uncomfortable with change.

- **Solution:**

  - **Change Management:** Implement change management strategies that address resistance at both the individual and organizational levels.

  - **Success Stories:** Share success stories from early DevOps adopters within the organization to inspire and motivate others.

9. Lack of Metrics and KPIs:

- **Challenge:** Without metrics and key performance indicators (KPIs), it's challenging to measure the impact of DevOps practices.

- **Solution:**

  - **Define Metrics:** Define relevant metrics and KPIs to measure the effectiveness of DevOps practices. Metrics may include deployment frequency, lead time, and change failure rate.

  - **Regular Review:** Regularly review and adapt metrics based on the evolving needs of the organization.

10. Coordination and Dependency Management:

- **Challenge:** In complex environments, managing dependencies between teams and systems can lead to bottlenecks and delays.

- **Solution:**

  - **Effective Coordination:** Implement effective coordination mechanisms, such as cross-team communication, shared calendars, and dependency tracking tools.

  - **Agile Frameworks:** Consider adopting agile frameworks like SAFe or LeSS to provide structure for large-scale coordination.

In conclusion, while DevOps adoption comes with its share of challenges, organizations can navigate and overcome these obstacles through a combination of cultural change, automation, effective communication, and the adoption of best practices. DevOps is a journey of continuous improvement, and as organizations evolve, they can fine-tune their strategies to ensure they reap the full benefits of DevOps in terms of agility, innovation, and reliability.

Conclusion

As we draw the final curtain on this journey through these pages, we invite you to reflect on the knowledge, insights, and discoveries that have unfolded before you. Our exploration of various subjects has been a captivating voyage into the depths of understanding.

In these chapters, we have ventured through the intricacies of numerous topics and examined the key concepts and findings that define these fields. It is our hope that you have found inspiration, enlightenment, and valuable takeaways that resonate with you on your own quest for knowledge.

Remember that the pursuit of understanding is an ever-evolving journey, and this book is but a milestone along the way. The world of knowledge is vast and boundless, offering endless opportunities for exploration and growth.

As you conclude this book, we encourage you to carry forward the torch of curiosity and continue your exploration of these subjects. Seek out new perspectives, engage in meaningful discussions, and embrace the thrill of lifelong learning.

We express our sincere gratitude for joining us on this intellectual adventure. Your curiosity and dedication to expanding your horizons are the driving forces behind our shared quest for wisdom and insight.

Thank you for entrusting us with a portion of your intellectual journey. May your pursuit of knowledge lead you to new heights and inspire others to embark on their own quests for understanding.

With profound gratitude,

Nikhilesh Mishra, Author

Recap of Key Takeaways

In this concluding section, we will revisit the essential insights and knowledge you've gained throughout your journey in "Mastering DevOps: Concepts, Techniques, and Applications." These key takeaways serve as a compass to navigate the vast terrain of DevOps concepts, practices, and technologies.

1. **DevOps Fundamentals:** DevOps is not just a set of tools; it's a cultural shift that promotes collaboration between development and operations teams. It emphasizes automation, continuous integration, and continuous deployment (CI/CD) for faster and more reliable software delivery.

2. **Continuous Integration (CI):** CI involves regularly integrating code changes into a shared repository, automating build and test processes, and detecting issues early in the development cycle.

3. **Continuous Deployment (CD):** CD takes CI a step further by automating the deployment process, allowing for rapid and reliable releases to production environments.

4. **Automation:** Automation is the backbone of DevOps. It reduces manual tasks, minimizes errors, and enhances efficiency throughout the software development lifecycle.

5. **Infrastructure as Code (IaC):** IaC enables the provisioning

and management of infrastructure using code, promoting consistency and scalability.

6. **Security in DevOps:** Security should be integrated from the start. DevSecOps practices embed security checks and compliance measures into the DevOps pipeline.

7. **Monitoring and Feedback:** Continuous monitoring and feedback loops are critical for identifying issues, measuring performance, and driving continuous improvement.

8. **Cloud and Multi-Cloud:** Cloud services offer scalability and flexibility for DevOps, but they also present unique challenges. Multi-cloud strategies help mitigate vendor lock-in.

9. **Advanced DevOps:** Explore advanced topics like DevOps in microservices architecture, DevOps for AI and machine learning, chaos engineering, and DevOps for mobile and IoT.

10. **DevOps Culture and Transformation:** Cultural transformation is a key component of DevOps success. Leadership, communication, and experimentation foster a culture of collaboration and learning.

11. **Real-world Implementations:** Case studies and success stories demonstrate how DevOps principles and practices have been applied in various industries and contexts.

12. **Challenges and Solutions:** Understand the common challenges in DevOps adoption and the solutions to overcome them.

Your Journey Continues

As you reflect on these key takeaways, remember that DevOps is not a static destination but a continuous journey. Embrace the principles of continuous improvement, experimentation, and collaboration as you apply DevOps practices in your own context.

We hope that "Mastering DevOps: Concepts, Techniques, and Applications" has equipped you with the knowledge, skills, and inspiration to excel in the world of DevOps. Your pursuit of mastery is a testament to your dedication and commitment to driving positive change in the world of technology.

Now, as you conclude this book, your journey in DevOps is far from over. The future holds limitless opportunities, and the skills and insights you've gained will serve as your compass on this ever-evolving path.

Thank you for joining us on this remarkable DevOps expedition. May your continued exploration lead to innovation, efficiency, and success in all your endeavors.

Sincerely,

Nikhilesh Mishra, Author

The Future of DevOps

DevOps has come a long way since its inception, and its future promises to be even more dynamic and transformative. Here are some key trends and developments that are shaping the future of DevOps:

1.   **AI and Automation:** Artificial intelligence (AI) and machine learning are becoming integral to DevOps. AI-powered tools can analyze vast amounts of data to identify patterns, predict issues, and automate decision-making. This leads to smarter, more autonomous DevOps processes, reducing manual intervention and enhancing efficiency.

2.   **GitOps:** GitOps is an emerging practice that extends the principles of Git version control to infrastructure and deployment. It emphasizes declarative definitions stored in Git repositories, enabling automated infrastructure updates and application deployments. GitOps simplifies the management of complex, distributed systems.

3.   **Serverless Computing:** Serverless architectures, such as AWS Lambda and Azure Functions, are gaining popularity. DevOps teams will need to adapt to this paradigm by focusing more on event-driven development and optimizing serverless functions for performance and cost-efficiency.

4.   **DevSecOps Maturity:** Security is a top concern in

DevOps. DevSecOps practices will continue to evolve, with security becoming an integral part of the entire software development lifecycle. Automation will play a key role in identifying and addressing security vulnerabilities early in the pipeline.

5.   **Edge Computing:** As edge computing gains prominence in IoT and real-time applications, DevOps practices will need to extend to the edge. Managing and deploying updates to edge devices and ensuring their reliability will become essential.

6.   **NoOps:** The concept of NoOps, where operations are so automated that they require little to no human intervention, is on the horizon. While complete NoOps may not be achievable in all scenarios, the trend toward minimizing manual operations tasks will continue.

7.   **Kubernetes and Beyond:** Kubernetes has become the de facto container orchestration platform. Its ecosystem is evolving rapidly, and DevOps teams will need to stay current with new features and tools. Beyond Kubernetes, innovations in containerization and orchestration may emerge.

8.   **Hybrid and Multi-Cloud Environments:** Organizations are increasingly adopting hybrid and multi-cloud strategies. DevOps practices will need to adapt to manage infrastructure and applications across multiple cloud providers

and on-premises environments seamlessly.

9.   **Shift Left and Shift Right Testing:** Testing practices will continue to shift earlier in the development process (Shift Left) to catch issues sooner. Additionally, "Shift Right" practices involve monitoring and testing in production to detect issues proactively.

10.   **DevOps Culture and Diversity:** DevOps culture will remain a critical aspect of success. Embracing diversity, inclusion, and a growth mindset will be essential for fostering innovation and collaboration within DevOps teams.

Adapting to the Future

To thrive in the future of DevOps, organizations and practitioners must remain adaptable and open to change. Continuous learning, experimentation, and the willingness to embrace new technologies and practices will be key. DevOps is not a destination but an ongoing journey, and those who navigate it with agility and foresight will be best positioned to succeed in the ever-evolving tech landscape.

In conclusion, the future of DevOps is one of continuous evolution, driven by technological advancements, changing business needs, and the relentless pursuit of efficiency and quality. As DevOps professionals, you are at the forefront of this transformation, shaping the way software is developed, delivered, and maintained. Embrace the challenges and opportunities that lie ahead, and let your commitment to DevOps excellence propel you into a future of innovation and success.

Glossary of Terms

This glossary provides definitions and explanations of essential terms, acronyms, and concepts used in the book. It serves as a quick reference guide to enhance your understanding of DevOps.

1.   **Agile:** An iterative and collaborative approach to software development that emphasizes adaptability, customer feedback, and cross-functional teams.

2.   **Automation:** The use of technology and scripts to perform tasks and processes without human intervention, a core principle in DevOps.

3.   **CI/CD (Continuous Integration/Continuous Deployment):** A DevOps practice of automating the integration, testing, and deployment of code changes, ensuring a rapid and reliable software delivery pipeline.

4.   **Containerization:** A technology that packages applications and their dependencies into isolated containers, enabling consistent deployment across different environments.

5.   **Docker:** A popular containerization platform that allows developers to package applications and dependencies into containers for easy deployment and scaling.

6.   **Git:** A distributed version control system used for tracking changes in source code during software development.

7. **Infrastructure as Code (IaC):** A practice of managing and provisioning infrastructure using code and automation tools like Terraform and Ansible.

8. **Kubernetes:** An open-source container orchestration platform for automating the deployment, scaling, and management of containerized applications.

9. **Microservices:** A software architectural approach that structures applications as a collection of small, loosely coupled services that can be developed, deployed, and scaled independently.

10. **Monitoring:** The process of collecting and analyzing data from systems and applications to ensure their health, performance, and availability.

11. **Orchestration:** The automated coordination and management of complex tasks and processes, often used in the context of containerized applications.

12. **Scalability:** The ability of a system to handle increased workloads by adding resources or scaling horizontally.

13. **Security in DevOps (DevSecOps):** Integrating security practices and controls into the DevOps pipeline to identify and address vulnerabilities early in the development process.

14. **Serverless Computing:** A cloud computing model where cloud providers automatically manage infrastructure, allowing developers to focus on code.

15. **Source Code Management:** The practice of tracking and managing changes to source code using version control systems like Git.

16. **Test Automation:** The use of automated scripts and tools to perform software testing, ensuring consistency and efficiency in testing processes.

17. **Workflow Automation:** The automation of workflows and processes, often used in DevOps to streamline development, testing, and deployment.

18. **Zero-Day Vulnerability:** A security vulnerability that is exploited before the software vendor is aware of it and can release a patch.

19. **Immutable Infrastructure:** An approach where infrastructure is not modified after deployment but replaced entirely when changes are required.

20. **Chaos Engineering:** A practice of intentionally introducing failures and disruptions into systems to identify weaknesses and improve resilience.

This glossary serves as a valuable reference as you navigate the world of DevOps. If you encounter any unfamiliar terms while reading this book, consult this glossary for clear and concise explanations.

Resources and References

As you reach the final pages of this book by Nikhilesh Mishra, consider it not an ending but a stepping stone. The pursuit of knowledge is an unending journey, and the world of information is boundless.

Discover a World Beyond These Pages

We extend a warm invitation to explore a realm of boundless learning and discovery through our dedicated online platform: **www.nikhileshmishra.com**. Here, you will unearth a carefully curated trove of resources and references to empower your quest for wisdom.

Unleash the Potential of Your Mind

- **Digital Libraries:** Immerse yourself in vast digital libraries, granting access to books, research papers, and academic treasures.

- **Interactive Courses:** Engage with interactive courses and lectures from world-renowned institutions, nurturing your thirst for knowledge.

- **Enlightening Talks:** Be captivated by enlightening talks delivered by visionaries and experts from diverse fields.

- **Community Connections:** Connect with a global community of like-minded seekers, engage in meaningful discussions, and share your knowledge journey.

Your Journey Has Just Begun

Your journey as a seeker of knowledge need not end here. Our website awaits your exploration, offering a gateway to an infinite universe of insights and references tailored to ignite your intellectual curiosity.

Acknowledgments

As I stand at this pivotal juncture, reflecting upon the completion of this monumental work, I am overwhelmed with profound gratitude for the exceptional individuals who have been instrumental in shaping this remarkable journey.

In Loving Memory

To my father, **Late Shri Krishna Gopal Mishra,** whose legacy of wisdom and strength continues to illuminate my path, even in his physical absence, I offer my deepest respect and heartfelt appreciation.

The Pillars of Support

My mother**, Mrs. Vijay Kanti Mishra,** embodies unwavering resilience and grace. Your steadfast support and unwavering faith in my pursuits have been the bedrock of my journey.

To my beloved wife, **Mrs. Anshika Mishra,** your unshakable belief in my abilities has been an eternal wellspring of motivation. Your constant encouragement has propelled me to reach new heights.

My daughter, **Miss Aarvi Mishra,** infuses my life with boundless joy and unbridled inspiration. Your insatiable curiosity serves as a constant reminder of the limitless power of exploration and discovery.

Brothers in Arms

To my younger brothers, **Mr. Ashutosh Mishra** and **Mr. Devashish Mishra,** who have steadfastly stood by my side, offering unwavering support and shared experiences that underscore the strength of familial bonds.

A Journey Shared

This book is a testament to the countless hours of dedication and effort that have gone into its creation. I am immensely grateful for the privilege of sharing my knowledge and insights with a global audience.

Readers, My Companions

To all the readers who embark on this intellectual journey alongside me, your curiosity and unquenchable thirst for knowledge inspire me to continually push the boundaries of understanding in the realm of cloud computing.

With profound appreciation and sincere gratitude,

Nikhilesh Mishra

September 17, 2023

About the Author

Nikhilesh Mishra is an extraordinary visionary, propelled by an insatiable curiosity and an unyielding passion for innovation. With a relentless commitment to exploring the boundaries of knowledge and technology, Nikhilesh has embarked on an exceptional journey to unravel the intricate complexities of our world.

Hailing from the vibrant and diverse landscape of India, Nikhilesh's pursuit of knowledge has driven him to plunge deep into the world of discovery and understanding from a remarkably young age. His unwavering determination and quest for innovation have not only cemented his position as a thought leader but have also earned him global recognition in the ever-evolving realm of technology and human understanding.

Over the years, Nikhilesh has not only mastered the art of translating complex concepts into accessible insights but has also crafted a unique talent for inspiring others to explore the limitless possibilities of human potential.

Nikhilesh's journey transcends the mere boundaries of expertise; it is a transformative odyssey that challenges conventional wisdom and redefines the essence of exploration. His commitment to pushing the boundaries and reimagining the norm serves as a luminous beacon of inspiration to all those who aspire to make a profound impact in the world of knowledge.

273

As you navigate the intricate corridors of human understanding and innovation, you will not only gain insight into Nikhilesh's expertise but also experience his unwavering dedication to empowering readers like you. Prepare to be enthralled as he seamlessly melds intricate insights with real-world applications, igniting the flames of curiosity and innovation within each reader.

Nikhilesh Mishra's work extends beyond the realm of authorship; it is a reflection of his steadfast commitment to shaping the future of knowledge and exploration. It is an embodiment of his boundless dedication to disseminating wisdom for the betterment of individuals worldwide.

Prepare to be inspired, enlightened, and empowered as you embark on this transformative journey alongside Nikhilesh Mishra. Your understanding of the world will be forever enriched, and your passion for exploration and innovation will reach new heights under his expert guidance.

Sincerely, **A Fellow Explorer**

Notes

Notes

Notes

Notes

Notes

Notes

Notes

Notes

Notes